Among t

by Clara Dᵢ ... ...ᵣson

CONTENTS

THE BIGGEST FROG AWAKENS

The Biggest Frog stretched the four toes of his right forefoot. Then he stretched the four toes of his left forefoot. Next he stretched the five toes of his right hindfoot. And last of all he stretched the four toes of his left hindfoot. Then he stretched all seventeen toes at once. He should have had eighteen toes to stretch, like his friends and neighbors, but something had happened to the eighteenth one a great many years before. None of the pond people knew what had happened to it, but something had, and when the Tadpoles teased him to tell them what, he only stared at them with his great eyes and said, "My children, that story is too sad to tell."

After the Biggest Frog had stretched all his toes, he stretched his legs and twitched his lips. He poked his head out of the mud a very, very little way, and saw a Minnow swimming past. "Good day!" said he. "Is it time to get up?"

"Time!" exclaimed the Minnow, looking at him with her mouth open. "I should say it was. Why, the watercress is growing!"

Now every one who lives in a pond knows that when the watercress begins to grow, it is time for all the winter sleepers to awaken. The Biggest Frog crawled out of the mud and poked this way and that all around the spot where he had spent the cold weather. "Wake up!" he said. "Wake up! Wake up!" The water grew dark and cloudy because he kicked up so much mud, but when it began to clear again he saw the heads of his friends peeping up everywhere out of that part of the pond bottom. Seven of them had huddled close to him all winter. "Come out!" he cried. "The spring is here, and it is no time for Frogs to be asleep."

"Asleep! No indeed!" exclaimed his sister, an elderly and hard-working Frog, as she swam to the shore and crawled out on it. She ate every bit of food that she found on the way, for neither she nor any of the others had taken a mouthful since the fall before.

The younger Frogs followed through the warmer shallow water until they were partly out of it. There is always a Biggest Frog in every pond. All the young Frogs thought how fine it would be to become the Biggest Frog of even a very small puddle, for then they could tell the others what to do. Now they looked at their leader and each said to himself, "Perhaps some day I shall begin the concert."

The Biggest Frog found a comfortable place and sat down. He toed in with his eight front toes, as well-bred frogs do, and all his friends toed in with their eight front toes. He toed out with his nine back toes, and all his friends toed out with their ten back toes. One young Yellow Brown Frog said, "How I wish I did not have that bothersome fifth toe on my left hindfoot! It is so in the way! Besides, there is such a style about having one's hind feet different." He spoke just loud enough for the Biggest Frog to hear. Any one would know from this remark that he was young and foolish, for when people are wise they know that the most beautiful feet and ears and bodies are just the way that they were first made to be.

Now the Biggest Frog swallowed a great deal of air, filled the sacs on each side of his neck with it, opened his big mouth, and sang croakily, "Frogs! Frogs! Frogs! Frogs! Frogs! Frogs! Frogs! Frogs!" And all the others sang, "Frogs! Frogs! Frogs!" as long as he. The Gulls heard it, and the Muskrats heard it, and all were happy because spring had come.

A beautiful young Green Brown Frog, who had never felt grown-up until now, tried to sing with the others, but she had not a strong voice, and was glad enough to stop and visit with the Biggest Frog's Sister. "Don't you wish we could sing as loudly as they can?" said she.

"No," answered the Biggest Frog's Sister. "I would rather sit on the bank and think about my spring work. Work first, you know, and pleasure afterward!"

"Oh!" said the Green Brown Frog. "Then you don't want to sing until your work is done?"

"You may be very sure I don't want to sing then," answered the older Frog. "I am too tired. Besides, after the eggs are laid, there is no reason for wanting to sing."

"Why not?" asked the Green Brown Frog. "I don't see what difference that makes."

"That," said the older Frog wisely, "is because you are young and have never laid eggs. The great time for singing is before the eggs are laid. There is some singing afterward, but that is only because people expect it of us, and not because we have the same wish to sing." After she had said all this, which was a great deal for a Frog to say at once, she shut her big mouth and slid her eyelids over her eyes.

There was another question which the Green Brown Frog wanted very much to ask, but she had good manners and knew that it was impolite to speak to any Frog whose eyes were not open. So she closed her own eyes and tried to think what the answer would be. When she opened them again, the Biggest Frog's Sister had hopped away, and in her place sat the Yellow Brown Frog, the same handsome young fellow who had found one of his toes in the way. It quite startled her to find him sitting so close to her and she couldn't think of anything to say, so she just looked at him with her great beautiful eyes and toed in a little more with her front feet. That made him look at them and see how pretty they were, although of course this was not the reason why she had moved them.

The Yellow Brown Frog hopped a little nearer and sang as loudly as he could, "Frogs! Frogs! Frogs! Frogs! Frogs! Frogs! Frogs! Frogs!" Then she knew that he was singing just for her, and she was exceedingly happy. She swallowed air very fast because she seemed to be out of breath from thinking what she should answer. She had wanted to ask the Biggest Frog's Sister what she should say if any one sang to her alone. She knew that if she wanted to get away from him, all she had to do was to give a great jump and splash into the water. She didn't want to go away, yet she made believe that she did, for she hopped a little farther from him.

He knew she was only pretending, though, for she hadn't hopped more than the length of a grass-blade. So he followed her and kept on singing. Because she knew that she must say something, she just opened her mouth and sang the first words that she could think of; and what she sang was, "Eggs! Eggs! Eggs! Eggs! Eggs! Eggs! Eggs! Eggs!" As it happened, this was exactly what she should have sung, so he knew that she liked him. They stayed together for a long, long time, and he sang a great deal and very loudly, and she sang a little and very softly.

After a while she remembered that she was now a fully grown Frog and had spring work to do, and she said to him, "I really must lay some eggs. I am going into the water."

"Then I will go too," said he. And they gave two great leaps and came down with two great splashes.

The Green Brown Frog laid eggs for four days, and the Yellow Brown Frog stayed with her all that time and took care of the eggs after she had laid them. They were covered with a sort of green jelly which made them stick to each other as they floated in little heaps on the water. The Frogs thought that a good thing, for then, when the Tadpoles hatched, each would have playmates near.

One day, after the eggs were all laid and were growing finely (for Frogs' eggs grow until the Tadpoles are ready to eat their way out), the Green Brown Frog sat alone on the bank of the pond and the Biggest Frog's Sister came to her. She had a queer smile around the corners of her mouth. Frogs have excellent mouths for smiling, but it takes a very broad smile to go way across, so when they smile a little it is only at the corners. "How are your eggs growing?" she asked.

"Oh," answered the Green Brown Frog sadly, "I can't tell which ones they are."

"That's just like a young Frog," said the Biggest Frog's Sister. "Is there any reason why you should know which ones they are? It isn't as though you were a bird and had to keep them warm, or as though you were a Mink and had to feed your children. The sun will hatch them and they will feed themselves all they need."

"I think," said the Green Brown Frog, "that my eggs were a little better than the rest."

"Yes," croaked the Biggest Frog's Sister, "every Frog thinks that."

"And I wanted to have my own Tadpoles to look after," sighed the Green Brown Frog.

"Why?" asked the Biggest Frog's Sister. "Can't you take any comfort with a Tadpole unless you laid the egg from which he was hatched? I never know one of my own eggs a day after it is laid. There are such a lot floating around that they are sure to get mixed. But I just make the best of it."

"How?" asked the Green Brown Frog, looking a little more cheerful.

"Oh, I swim around and look at all the eggs, and whenever I see any Tadpoles moving in them I think, 'Those may be mine!' As they are hatched I help any one who needs it. Poor sort of Frog it would be who couldn't like other people's Tadpoles!"

"I believe I'll do that way," said the Green Brown Frog. "And then," she added, "what a comfort it will be if any of them are cross or rude, to think, 'I'm glad I don't know that they are mine.'"

"Yes," said the Biggest Frog's Sister. "I often tell my brother that I pity people who have to bring up their own children. It is much pleasanter to let them grow up as they do and then adopt the best ones. Do you know, I have almost decided that you are my daughter? My brother said this morning that he thought you looked like me."

THE DANCE OF THE SAND-HILL CRANES

One fine day in spring, a great flock of Sand-hill Cranes came from the south. They were flying high and quietly because the weather was bright. If it had been stormy, or if they had been flying by night, as they usually did, they would have stayed nearer the ground, and their leader would have trumpeted loudly to let his followers know which way he was going. They would also have trumpeted, but more softly, to tell him that they were coming after.

They were a fine company to look upon, orderly, strong, and dignified. Their long necks were stretched out straight ahead, their long legs straight behind, and they beat the air with slow, regular strokes of the strong wings. As they came near the pond, they flew lower and lower, until all swept down to the earth and alighted, tall and stately, by the edge of the water.

They had eaten nothing for several days, and were soon hunting for food, some on land, and some in the water, for they had stopped to feed and rest. Those who hunted in the water, did so very quietly. A Crane would stand on one leg, with his head against his breast, so quietly that one might think him asleep: but as soon as anything eatable came near, he would bend his body, stretch out his neck, open his long, slender bill, and swallow it at one gulp. Then he would seem to fall asleep again.

While most of the Cranes were still feeding, some of them were stalking through the woods and looking this way and that, flying up to stand on a tree, and then flying down to stand on the ground. They were those who thought of staying there for the summer.

When the flock arose to fly on again, eight Cranes stayed behind. They watched their friends fly away, and stood on the ground with their necks and bills uplifted and mouths open, while they trumpeted or called out, "Good-bye! Stop for us in the fall!" The flying Cranes trumpeted back, "We will! Don't forget us!"

That night they slept near together, as they had done when with the large flock, and one Crane kept awake to watch for danger while the others tucked their heads under their wings. They were fine looking, even when they slept, and some people never look well unless they are awake. They were brownish-gray, with no bright markings at all, and their long legs gave them a very genteel look. The tops of their heads were covered with warty red skin, from which grew short black feathers that looked more like hairs.

One morning, when the Cranes awakened, a fine young fellow began to strut up and down before the rest, bowing low, and leaping high into the air, and every now and then whooping as loudly as he could. The Gulls, who had spent the winter by the pond, screamed to each other, "The Crane dance has begun!" Even the Frogs, who are afraid of Cranes, crept quietly near to look on.

It was not long before another young Crane began to skip and hop and circle around, drooping his wings and whooping as he went. Every Crane danced, brothers, and sisters, and all, and as they did so, they looked lovingly at each other, and admired the fine steps and enjoyed the whooping. This went on until they were so tired they could hardly stand, and had to stop to eat and rest.

When they were eating, the young fellow who had begun the dance, stalked up to the sister of one of his friends, as she stood in the edge of the pond, gracefully balanced on one leg. She did not turn her head towards him, although, having such a long and slender neck, she could have done so with very little trouble. She stood with her head on her breast and looked at the water. After a while, he trumpeted softly, as though he were just trying his voice. Then she gave a pretty little start, and said, "Oh, are you here? How you did frighten me!"

"I am sorry," he said. "I did not want to frighten you." And he looked at her admiringly.

"It was just for a minute," she answered. "Of course I am not frightened now that I know who it is."

Then they stood and fished for a long time without saying anything. When she flew away, she said, "That is a very pleasant fishing-place." He stood on the other leg for a while, and thought how sweet her voice sounded as she said it. Then he thought that, if she liked the place so well, she might come there again the next day. He wondered why he could not come too, although everybody knows that a Crane catches more if he fishes alone.

The next morning, when the Cranes danced, he bowed to her oftener than to any of the rest, and he thought she noticed it. They danced until they were almost too tired to move, and indeed he had to rest for a while before he went to feed. As she stalked off toward the pond, she passed him, and she said over her shoulder, "I should think you would be hungry. I am almost starved." After she had gone, he wondered why she had said that. If he had been an older Crane, and understood the ways of the world a little better, he would have known that she meant, "Aren't you coming to that fishing-place? I am going now." Still, although he was such a young Crane and had never danced until this year, he began to think that she liked him and enjoyed having him near. So he flew off to the fishing-place where he had seen her the day before, and he stalked along to where she was, and stood close to her while she fished. Once, when he caught something and swallowed it at one gulp, she looked admiringly at him and said, "What fine, big mouthfuls you can take!"

That pleased him, of course, because Cranes think that big mouthfuls are the best kind, so he tipped his head to one side, and watched his neck as the mouthful slid down to his stomach. He could see it from the outside, a big bunch slowly moving downward. He often did this while he was eating. He thought it very interesting. He pitied short-necked people. Then he said, "Pooh! I can take bigger mouthfuls than that. You ought to see what big mouthfuls I can take."

She changed, and stood on her other leg. "I saw you dancing this morning," she said. Now it was not at all queer that she should have seen him dancing, for all the eight Cranes had danced together, but he thought it very wonderful.

"Did you notice to whom I bowed?" he asked. He was so excited that his knees shook, and he had to stand on both legs at once to keep from falling. When a Crane is as much excited as that, it is pretty serious.

"To my sister?" she asked carelessly, as she drew one of her long tail-feathers through her beak.

"No," said he. "I bowed to her sister." He thought that was a very clever thing to say. But she suddenly raised her head, and said, "There! I have forgotten something," and flew off, as she had done the day before. He wondered what it was. Long afterward he asked her what she had forgotten and she said she couldn't remember--that she never could remember what she had forgotten.

It made him feel very badly to have her leave him so. He wanted a chance to tell her something, yet, whenever he tried to, it seemed to stick in his bill. He began to fear that she didn't like him; and the next time the Cranes danced he didn't bow to her so much, but he strutted and leaped and whooped even more. And she strutted and leaped and whooped almost as loudly as he. When they were all tired out and had stopped dancing, she said to him, "I am so tired! Let us go off into the woods and rest."

You may be very sure he was glad to go, and as he stalked off with her, he led the way to a charming nesting-place. He didn't know just how to tell what he wanted to, but he had seen another Crane bowing to her, and was afraid she might marry him if he was not quick. Now he pointed with one wing to this nesting-place, and said, "How would you like to build a nest there?"

She looked where he had pointed, "I?" she said. "Why, it is a lovely place, but I could never have a nest alone."

"Let me help you," he said. "I want to marry and have a home."

"Why," said she, as she preened her feathers, "that is a very good plan. When did you think of it?"

So they were married, and Mrs. Sand-Hill Crane often told her friends afterward that Mr. Crane was so much in love with her that she just had to marry him. They were very, very happy, and after a while--but that is another story.

THE YOUNG MINNOW WHO WOULD NOT EAT WHEN HE SHOULD

"When I grow up," said one young Minnow, "I am going to be a Bullhead, and scare all the little fishes."

"I'm not," said his sister. "I'm going to be a Sucker, and lie around in the mud."

"Lazy! Lazy!" cried the other young Minnows, wiggling their front fins at her.

"What is the matter?" asked a Father Minnow, swimming in among them with a few graceful sweeps of his tail, and stopping himself by spreading his front fins. He had the beautiful scarlet coloring on the under part of his body which Father Minnows wear in the summer-time. That is, most of them do, but some wear purple. "What is the matter?" he asked again, balancing himself with his top fin and his two hind ones.

Then all the little Minnows spoke at once. "He says that when he grows up he is going to be a Bullhead, and frighten all the small fishes; and she says that she is going to be a Sucker, and lie around in the mud; and we say that Suckers are lazy, and they are lazy, aren't they?"

"I am surprised at you," began the Father Minnow severely, "to think that you should talk such nonsense. You ought to know----"

But just then a Mother Minnow swam up to him. "The Snapping Turtle is looking for you," she said. Father Minnow hurried away and she turned to the little ones. "I heard what you were saying," she remarked, with a twinkle in her flat, round eyes. "Which of you is going to be a Wild Duck? Won't somebody be a Frog?" She had had more experience in bringing up children than Father Minnow, and she didn't scold so much. She did make fun of them though, sometimes; and you can do almost anything with a young Minnow if you love him a great deal and make fun of him a little.

"Why-ee!" said the young Minnows. "We wouldn't think of being Wild Ducks, and we couldn't be Frogs, you know. Frogs have legs--four of them. A fish couldn't be a Frog if he wanted to!"

"No," said Mother Minnow. "A fish cannot be anything but a fish, and a Minnow cannot be anything but a Minnow. So if you will try to be just as good Minnows as you can, we will let the little Bullheads and Suckers do their own growing up."

She looked at them all again with her flat, round eyes, which saw so much and were always open, because there was nothing to make them shut. She saw one tiny fellow hiding behind his brother. "Have you torn your fin again?" she asked.

"Yes'm, just a little," said he. "A boy caught me when he was in wading, and I tore it when I flopped away from him."

"Dreadful!" said she. "How you do look! If you are so careless, you will soon not have a whole fin to your back--or your front either. Children, you must remember to swim away from boys. When the Cows wade in to drink, you may stay among them, if you wish. They are friendly. We pond people are afraid of boys, although some of them are said not to be dangerous."

"Pooh!" said one young Minnow. "All the pond people are not so afraid! The Bloodsuckers say they like them."

The Mother Minnow looked very severe when he said this, but she only replied, "Very well. When you are a Bloodsucker you may stay near boys. As long as you are a Minnow, you must stay away."

"Now," she added, "swim along, the whole school of you! I am tired and want a nap in the pondweed." So they all swam away, and she wriggled her silvery brown body into the soft green weeds and had a good sleep. She was careful to hide herself, for there were some people in the pond whom she did not want to have find her; and, being a fish, she could not hear very distinctly if they came near. Of course her eyes were open even when she was asleep, because she had no eyelids, but they were not working although they were open. That is an uncomfortable thing about being a fish--one cannot hear much. One cannot taste much either, or feel much, yet when one has always been a fish and is used to it, it is not so hard.

She slept a long time, and then the whole school of young Minnows came to look for her. "We are afraid," they cried. "We feel so very queerly. We don't know how we feel, either, and that is the worst part of it. It might be in our stomachs, or it might be in our fins, and perhaps there is something wrong with our gill-covers. Wake up and tell us what is the matter."

The Mother Minnow awakened and she felt queerly too, but, being older, she knew what was the matter. "That," she said, "is the storm feeling."

"But," said the young Minnows, "there isn't any storm."

"No," she answered wisely. "Not now."

"And there hasn't been any," they said.

"No," she answered again. "The storm you feel is the storm that is going to be."

"And shall we always feel it so?" they asked.

"Always before a storm," she said.

"Why?" asked the young Minnows.

"Because," said she. "There is no answer to that question, but just 'because.' When the storm comes you cannot smell your food and find it, so you must eat all you can before then. Eat everything you can find and be quick." As she spoke she took a great mouthful of pondweed and swallowed it.

All but one of the young Minnows swam quickly away to do as she had told them to. This young Minnow wanted to know just how and why and all about it, so he stayed to ask questions. You know there are some questions which fishes cannot answer, and some which Oxen cannot answer, and some which nobody can answer; and when the Mother Minnow told the young Minnows what she did, she had nothing more to tell. But there are some young Minnows who never will be satisfied, and who tease, and tease, and tease, and tease.

"Hurry along and eat all you can," said the Mother Minnow to him again.

"I want to know," said he, opening his mouth very wide indeed and breathing in a great deal of water as he spoke, "I want to know where I feel queerly."

"I can't tell," said the Mother Minnow, between mouthfuls. "No fish can tell."

"Well, what makes me feel queerly there?"

"The storm," said she.

"How does it make me feel queerly?"

"I don't know," said the Mother Minnow.

"Who does know?" asked the young Minnow.

"Nobody," said she, swallowing some more pondweed of one kind and then beginning on another. "Do eat something or you will be very hungry by and by."

"Well, why does a storm make me feel so?" asked he.

"Because!" said she. She said it very firmly and she was quite right in saying it then, for there was a cause, yet she could not tell what it was. There are only about seven times in one's life when it is right to answer in this way, and what the other six are you must decide for yourself.

Just then there was a peal of thunder which even a Minnow could hear, and the wind blew until the slender forest trees bent far over. The rain came down in great drops which pattered on the water of the pond and started tiny circles around each drop, every circle spreading wider and wider until it touched other circles and broke. Down in the darkened water the fishes lay together on the bottom, and wondered how long it would last, and hoped it would not be a great, great while before they could smell their food again.

One little fellow was more impatient than the others. "Didn't you eat enough to last you?" they said.

"I didn't eat anything," he answered.

"Not anything!" they exclaimed. "Why not?"

"Because!" said he. And that was not right, for he did know the reason. His mother looked at him, and he looked at her, and she had a twinkle in her round, flat eyes. "Poor child!" she thought. "He must be hungry." But she said nothing.

THE STICKLEBACK FATHER

Nobody can truthfully say that the Sticklebacks are not good fathers. There are no other fish fathers who work so hard for their children as the Sticklebacks do. As to the Stickleback Mothers--well, that is different.

This particular Stickleback Father had lived, ever since he had left the nest, with a little company of his friends in a quiet place near the edge of the pond. Sometimes, when they tired of staying quietly at home, they had made short journeys up a brook that emptied into the pond. It was a brook that flowed gently over an even bed, else they would never have gone there, for Sticklebacks like quiet waters. When they swam in this little stream, they met the Brook Trout, who were much larger than they, and who were the most important people there.

Now this Stickleback was a year old and knew much more than he did the summer before. When the alder tassels and pussy willows hung over the edge of the pond in the spring-time, he began to think seriously of life. He was no longer really young, and the days were past in which he was contented to just swim and eat and sleep. It was time he should build a home and raise a family if he wanted to ever be a grandfather. He had a few relatives who were great-grandfathers, and one who was a great-great-grandfather. That does not often happen, because to be a Stickleback Great-great-grandfather, one must be four years old, and few Sticklebacks live to that age.

As he began to think about these things, he left the company of his friends and went to live by himself. He chose a place near the edge of the pond to be his home; and he brushed the pond-bottom there with his tail until he had swept away all the loose sticks and broken shells. He told some Pond Snails, who were there, that they must move away because he wanted the place. At first they didn't want to go, but when they saw how fierce he looked, they thought about it again and decided that perhaps there were other places which would suit them quite as well--indeed, they might find one that they liked even better. Besides, as one of them said to his brother, they had to remember that in ponds it is always right for the weak people to give up to the strong people.

"It will take us quite a while to move," they said to him, "for you know we cannot hurry, but we will begin at once."

All the rest of that day each Snail was lengthening and shortening his one foot, which was his only way of walking. You can see how slow that must be, for a Snail cannot lift his foot from one place and put it down in another, or he would have nothing to stand on while he was lifting it. This was a very hard day for them, yet they were cheerful and made the best of it.

"Well," said one, as he stopped to rest his foot, "I'm glad we don't have to build a home when we do find the right place. How I pity people who have to do that!"

"Yes," said his brother. "There are not many so sure of their homes as we. And what people want of so much room, I can't understand! A Muskrat told me he wanted room to turn around in his house. I don't see what use there is in turning round, do you?"

"No," answered the other Snail, beginning to walk again. "It is just one of his silly ideas. My shell is big enough to let me draw in my whole body, and that is house room enough for any person!"

The Stickleback had not meant to look fierce at the Pond Snails. He had done so because he couldn't help it. All his fins were bristling with sharp points of bone, and he had extra bone-points sticking out of his back, besides wearing a great many of his flat bones on the outside. All his family had these extra bones, and that was why they were called Sticklebacks. They were a brave family and not afraid of many things, although they were so small. There came a time when the Stickleback Father wanted to look fierce, but that was later. Now he went to work to build his nest.

First he made a little hollow in the pond-bottom, and lined it with watergrass and tiny pieces of roots. Next, he made the side-walls of the same things, and last of all, the roof. When it was done, he swam carefully into it and looked around. Under and beside and over him were soft grasses and roots. At each end was an open doorway. "It is a good nest," he said, "a very good nest for my first one. Now I must ask some of my friends to lay eggs in it for me."

Before doing this, he went to look at the homes built by his neighbors. After he left the company in the quiet pool, many others did the same, until the only Sticklebacks left there were the dull-colored ones, the egg-layers. The nest-builders had been dull-colored, too, but in the spring-time there came beautiful red and blue markings on their bodies, until now they were very handsome fellows. It is sad to tell, still it is true, that they also became very cross at this time. Perhaps it was the work and worry of nest-building that made them so, yet, whatever it was, every bright-colored Stickleback wanted to fight every other bright-colored Stickleback. That was how it happened that, when this one went to look at the nest of an old friend, with whom he had played ever since he was hatched, this same friend called out, "Don't you come near my nest!"

The visiting Stickleback replied, "I shall if I want to!" Then they swam at each other and flopped and splashed and pushed and jabbed until both were very tired and sore, and each was glad to stay by his own home. This was the time when they wanted to look fierce.

[Illustration: THEN THEY SWAM AT EACH OTHER. Page 39]

Soon the dull-colored Sticklebacks came swimming past, waving their tails gracefully, and talking to each other. Now this fine fellow, who had sent the Snails away and built his nest, who had fought his old friend and come home again, swam up to a dull-colored Stickleback, and said, "Won't you lay a few eggs in my nest? I'm sure you will find it comfortable."

She answered, "Why, yes! I wouldn't mind laying a few there." And she tried to look as though she had not expected the invitation. While she was carefully laying the eggs in the nest, he stood ready to fight anybody who disturbed her. She came out after a while and swam away. Before she went, she said, "Aren't you ashamed to fight so? We dull-colored ones never fight."

She held her fins very stiff as she spoke, because she thought it her duty to scold him. The dull-colored Sticklebacks often did this. They thought that they were a little better than the others; so they swam around together and talked about things, and sometimes forgot how hard it was to be the nest-builder and stay at home and work. Then they called upon the bright-colored Sticklebacks, for they really liked them very much, and told them what they should do. That was why this one said, "We dull-colored ones never fight."

"Have you ever been red and blue?" asked the nest-builder.

"N--no," said she. "But I don't see what difference that makes."

"Well, it does make a difference," said he. "When a fellow is red and blue, he can't help fighting. I'll be as good-natured as any of you after I stop being red and blue."

Of course she could not say anything more after that, so she swam off to her sisters. The bright-colored Stickleback looked at the eggs she had laid. They were sticky, like the eggs of all fishes, so that they stuck to the bottom of the nest. He covered them carefully, and after that he was really a Stickleback Father. It is true that he did not have any Stickleback children to swim around him and open their dear little mouths at him, but he knew that the eggs would hatch soon, and that after he had built a nest and covered the eggs in it, the tiny Sticklebacks were beginning to grow.

However, he wanted more eggs in his nest, so he watched for another dull-colored Stickleback and called her in to help him. He did this until he had almost an hundred eggs there, and all this time he had fought every bright-colored Stickleback who came near him. He became very tired indeed; but he had to fight, you know, because he was red and blue. And he had covered all the eggs and guarded them, else they would never have hatched.

The dull-colored Sticklebacks were also tired. They had been swimming from nest to nest, laying a few eggs in each. Now they went off together to a quiet pool and ate everything they could find to eat, and visited with each other, and said it was a shame that the bright-colored Sticklebacks had fought so, and told how they thought little Sticklebacks should be brought up.

And now the red and blue markings on the Stickleback Father grew paler and paler, until he did not have to fight at all, and could call upon his friends and see how their children were hatching. One fine day, his first child broke the shell, and then another and another, until he had an hundred beautiful Stickleback babies to feed. He worked hard for them, and some nights, when he could stop and rest, his fins ached as though they would drop off. But they never did.

As the Stickleback children grew stronger, they swam off to take care of themselves, and he had less to do. When the last had gone, he left the old nest and went to the pool where the dull-colored Sticklebacks were. They told him he was not looking well, and that he hadn't managed the children right, and that they thought he tried to do too much.

He was too tired to talk about it, so he just said, "Perhaps," and began to eat something. Yet, down in his fatherly heart he knew it was worth doing. He knew, too, that when spring should come once more, he would become red and blue again, and build another nest, and fight and work and love as he had done before. "There is nothing in the world better than working for one's own little Sticklebacks," said he.

THE CARELESS CADDIS WORM

When the Caddis Fly felt like laying eggs, she crawled down the stalk of one of the pond plants and laid them there. She covered them with something sticky, so that they were sure to stay where she put them. "There!" she said, as she crawled up to the air again. "My work is done." Soon after this, she lay down for a long, long rest. What with flying, and visiting, and laying eggs, she had become very tired; and it was not strange, for she had not eaten a mouthful since she got her wings.

This had puzzled the Dragon-Flies very much. They could not understand it, because they were always eating. They would have liked to ask her about it, but they went to sleep for the night soon after she got up, and whenever she saw them coming she flew away. "I do not seem to feel hungry," said she, "so why should I eat? Besides," she added, "I couldn't eat if I wanted to, my mouth is so small and weak. I ate a great deal while I was growing--quite enough to last me--and it saves time not to bother with hunting food now."

When her eggs hatched, the larvae were slender, soft, six-footed babies called Caddis Worms. They were white, and they showed as plainly in the water as a pond-lily does on the top of it. It is not safe to be white if one is to live in the water; certainly not unless one can swim fast and turn quickly. And there is a reason for this, as any one of the pond people will tell you. Even the fishes wear all their white on the under side of their bodies, so that if they swim near the top of the water, a hungry Fish Hawk is not so likely to see them and pounce down on them.

The Caddis Worms soon found that white was not a good color to wear, and they talked of it among themselves. They were very bright larvae. One day the biggest one was standing on a stem of pickerel-weed, when his sister came toward him. She did not come very fast, because she was neither swimming nor walking, but biting herself along. All the Caddis Worms did this at times, for their legs were weak. She reached as far forward as she could, and fastened her strong jaws in the weed, then she gave a jerk and pulled her body ahead. "It is a very good way to travel," said she, "and such a saving of one's legs." Now she was in so great a hurry that sometimes when she pulled herself ahead, she turned a half-somersault and came down on her back.

"What is the matter?" called the Biggest Caddis Worm. "Don't hurry so. There is lots of time." That was just him, for he was lazy. Everybody said so.

"I must hurry," said she, and she breathed very fast with the white breathing hairs that grew on both sides of her body. She picked herself up from her last somersault and stood beside her brother, near enough to speak quite softly. "I have been getting away from Belostoma," she said, "and I was dreadfully afraid he would catch me."

"Well, you're all right now, aren't you?" asked her brother. And that was also like him. As long as he could have enough to eat and was comfortable, he did not want to think about anything unpleasant.

"No, I'm not," she answered, "and I won't be so long as any hungry fish or water-bug can see me so plainly. I'm tired of being white."

"You are not so white as you were," said her brother. "None of us children are. Our heads and the front part of our bodies are turning brown and getting harder." That was true, and he was particularly hard-headed.

"Yes, but what about the rest of us?" said she, and surely there was some excuse for her if she was impatient. "If Belostoma can see part of me and chase that, he will find the rest of me rather near by."

"Keep quiet then, and see if you don't get hard and brown all over," said he.

"I never shall," said she. "I went to the Clams and asked them if I would, and they said 'No.' I'm going to build a house to cover the back part of my body, and you'd better do the same thing."

The Biggest Caddis Worm looked very much surprised. "Whatever made you think of that?" said he.

"I suppose because there wasn't anything else to think of," said she. "One has to think of something."

"I don't," said he.

She started away to where her other brothers and sisters were. "Where are you going?" cried he.

"Going to build my house," answered she. "You'd better come too."

"Not now," said he. "I am waiting to get the rest of my breakfast. I'll come by and by."

The Biggest Caddis Worm stood on the pickerel-weed and ate his breakfast. Then he stood there a while longer. "I do not think it is well to work right after eating," he said. Below him in the water, his brothers and sisters were busily gathering tiny sticks, stones, and bits of broken shell, with which to make their houses. Each Caddis Worm found his own, and fastened them together with a sort of silk which he pulled out of his body. They had nobody to show them how, so each planned to suit himself, and no two were exactly alike.

"I'm going to make my house big enough so I can pull in my head and legs when I want to," said one.

"So am I," cried all the other Caddis Worms.

After a while, somebody said, "I'm going to have an open door at the back of my house." Then each of his busy brothers and sisters cried, "So am I."

When the tiny houses were done, each Caddis Worm crawled inside of his own, and lay with head and legs outside the front door. The white part of their bodies did not show at all, and, if they wanted to do so, they could pull their heads in. Even Belostoma, the Giant Water-Bug, might have passed close to them then and not seen them at all.

"Let's hook ourselves in!" cried one Caddis Worm, and all the others answered, "Let's."

So each hooked himself in with the two stout hooks which grew at the end of his body, and there they were as snug and comfortable as Clams. About this time the Big Brother came slowly along the stem of pickerel-weed. "What," said he, "you haven't got your houses done already?"

"Yes," answered the rest joyfully. "See us pull in our heads." And they all pulled in their heads and poked them out again. He was the only white-bodied person in sight.

"I must have a home," said he. "I wish one of you Worms would give me yours. You could make yourself another, you know. There is lots more stuff."

"Make it yourself," they replied. "Help yourself to stuff."

"But I don't know how," he said, "and you do."

"Whose fault is that?" asked his sister. Then she was afraid that he might think her cross, and she added quickly, "We'll tell you how, if you'll begin."

The Biggest Caddis Worm got together some tiny sticks and stones and pieces of broken shell, but it wasn't very much fun working alone. Then they told him what to do, and how to fasten them to each other with silk. "Be sure you tie them strongly," they said.

"Oh, that's strong enough," he answered. "It'll do, anyhow. If it comes to pieces I can fix it." His brothers and sisters thought he should make it stouter, yet they said nothing more, for he would not have liked it if they had; and they had already said so once. When he crawled into his house and hooked himself in, there was not a Caddis Worm in sight, and they were very proud to think how they had planned and built their houses. They did not know that Caddis Worms had always done so, and they thought themselves the first to ever think of such a thing.

The Biggest Caddis Worm's house was not well fastened together, and every day he said, "I really must fix it to-morrow." But when to-morrow came, it always proved to be to-day, and, besides, he usually found something more interesting to be done. It took him a great deal of time to change his skin, and that could not be easily put off. He grew so fast that he was likely to awaken almost any morning and find his head poking through the top of his skin, and, lazy as he was, he would not have the pond people see him around with a crack in the skin of his head, right where it showed. So when this happened, he always pulled his body through the crack, and threw the old skin away. There was sure to be a whole new one underneath, you know.

When they had changed their skin many times, the Caddis Worms became more quiet and thoughtful. At last the sister who had first planned to build houses, fastened hers to a stone, and spun gratings across both its front and its back doors. "I am going to sleep," she said, "to grow my feelers and get ready to fly and breathe air. I don't want anybody to awaken me. All I want to do is to sleep and grow and breathe. The water will come in through the gratings, so I shall be all right. I couldn't sleep in a house where there was not plenty of fresh water to breathe." Then she cuddled down and dozed off, and when her brothers and sisters spoke of her, they called her "the Caddis Nymph."

They did not speak of her many times, however, for they soon fastened their houses to something solid, and spun gratings in their doorways and went to sleep.

One day a Water-Adder came around where all the Caddis houses were. "Um-hum," said he to himself. "There used to be a nice lot of Caddis Worms around here, and now I haven't seen one in ever so long. I suppose they are hidden away somewhere asleep. Well, I must go away from here and find my dinner. I am nearly starved. The front half of my stomach hasn't a thing in it." He whisked his tail and went away, but that whisk hit a tiny house of sticks, stones, and bits of broken shell, and a fat sleeping Caddis Nymph rolled out. It was the Biggest Brother.

Soon Belostoma, the Giant Water-Bug, came that way. "What is this?" he exclaimed, as he saw the sleeping Caddis Nymph. "Somebody built a poor house to sleep in. You need to be cared for, young Caddis." He picked up the sleeping Caddis Nymph in his stout forelegs and swam off. Nobody knows just what happened after that.

When the other Caddis Nymphs awakened, they bit through their gratings and had a good visit before they crawled out of the pond into their new home, the air. "Has anybody seen my biggest brother?" asked one Nymph of another, but everybody answered, "No."

Each looked all around with his two far-apart eyes, and then they decided that he must have awakened first and left the water before them. But you know that he could not have done so, because he could never be a Caddis Fly unless he finished the Nymph-sleep in his house, and he did not do that. He had stopped being a Caddis Worm when he turned into a Caddis Nymph. Nobody will ever know just what did become of him unless Belostoma tells-- and Belostoma is not likely to tell.

THE TADPOLE WHO WANTED TO BE GROWN-UP

It was a bright, warm April day when the First Tadpole of the season ate his way out of the jelly-covered egg in which he had come to life. He was a very tiny, dark brown fellow. It would be hard to tell just what he did look like, for there is nothing in the world that one Tadpole looks like unless it is another Tadpole. He had a very small head with a busy little mouth opening on the front side of it: just above each end of this mouth was a shining black eye, and on the lower side of his head was a very wiggly tail. Somewhere between his head and the tip of this were his small stomach and places for legs, but one could not see all that in looking at him. It seemed as if what was not head was tail, and what was not tail was head.

When the First Tadpole found himself free in the water, he swam along by the great green floating jelly-mass of Frogs' eggs, and pressed his face up close to first one egg and then another. He saw other Tadpoles almost as large as he, and they were wriggling inside their egg homes. He couldn't talk to them through the jelly-mass--he could only look at them, and they looked greenish because he saw them through green jelly. They were really dark brown, like him. He wanted them to come out to play with him and he tried to show them that it was more interesting where he was, so he opened and shut his hard little jaws very fast and took big Tadpole-mouthfuls of green jelly.

Perhaps it was seeing this, and perhaps it was because the warm sunshine made them restless--but for some reason the shut-in Tadpoles nibbled busily at the egg-covering and before long were in the water with their brother. They all looked alike, and nobody except that one particular Tadpole knew who had been the first to hatch. He never forgot it, and indeed why should he? If one has ever been the First Tadpole, he is quite sure to remember the loneliness of it all his life.

Soon they dropped to the bottom of the pond and met their neighbors. They were such little fellows that nobody paid much attention to them. The older pond people often seemed to forget that the Tadpoles heard what they said, and cared too. The Minnows swam in and out among them, and hit them with their fins, and slapped them with their tails, and called them "little-big-mouths," and the Tadpoles couldn't hit back because they were so little. The Minnows didn't hurt the Tadpoles, but they made fun of them, and even the smallest Minnow would swim away if a Tadpole tried to play with him.

Then the Eels talked among themselves about them. "I shall be glad," said one old Father Eel, "when these youngsters hide their breathing-gills and go to the top of the water."

"So shall I," exclaimed a Mother Eel. "They keep their tails wiggling so that it hurts my eyes to look at them. Why can't they lie still and be good?"

Now the Tadpoles looked at each other with their shining black eyes. "What are our breathing-gills?" they asked. "They must be these little things on the sides of our heads."

"They are!" cried the First Tadpole. "The Biggest Frog said so. But I don't see where we can hide them, because they won't come off. And how could we ever breathe water without them?"

"Hear the children talk," exclaimed the Green Brown Frog, who had come down to look the Tadpoles over and decide which were hers. "Why, you won't always want to breathe water. Before long you will have to breathe air by swallowing it, and then you cannot stay long under water. I must go now. I am quite out of breath. Good-bye!"

Then the Tadpoles looked again at each other. "She didn't tell us what to do with our breathing-gills," they said. One of the Tadpoles who had hatched last, swam up to the First Tadpole. "Your breathing-gills are not so large as mine," she said.

"They surely are!" he exclaimed, for he felt very big indeed, having been the first to hatch.

"Oh, but they are not!" cried all his friends. "They don't stick out as they used to." And that was true, for his breathing-gills were sinking into his head, and they found that this was happening to all the older Tadpoles.

The next day they began going to the top to breathe air, the oldest ones first, and so on until they were all there. They thought it much pleasanter than the bottom of the pond, but it was not so safe. There were more dangers to be watched for here, and some of the careless young Tadpoles never lived to be Frogs. It is sad, yet it is always so.

Sometimes the Frogs came to see them, and once--once, after the Tadpoles had gotten their hindlegs, the Biggest Frog sat in the marsh near by and told them stories of his Tadpolehood. He said that he was always a very good little Tadpole, and always did as the Frogs told him to do; and that he was such a promising little fellow that every Mother Frog in the pond was sure that he had been hatched from one of her eggs.

"And were you?" asked one Tadpole, who never listened carefully, and so was always asking stupid questions.

The Biggest Frog looked at him very sternly. "No," said he, "I was not. Each wanted me as her son, but I never knew to which I belonged. I never knew! Still," he added, "it does not so much matter who a Frog's mother is, if the Frog is truly great." Then he filled the sacs on each side of his neck with air, and croaked loudly. His sister afterward told the Tadpoles that he was thinking of one of the forest people, the Ground Hog, who was very proud because he could remember his grandfather.

The Green Brown Frog came often to look at them and see how they were growing. She was very fond of the First Tadpole. "Why, you have your forelegs!" she exclaimed one morning. "How you do grow!"

"What will I have next?" he asked, "more legs or another tail?"

The Green Brown Frog smiled the whole length of her mouth, and that was a very broad smile indeed. "Look at me," she said. "What change must come next to make you look like a Frog?"

"You haven't any tail," he said slowly. "Is that all the difference between us Tadpoles and Frogs?"

"That is all the difference now," she answered, "but it will take a long, long time for your tail to disappear. It will happen with that quite as it did with your breathing-gills. You will grow bigger and bigger and bigger, and it will grow smaller and smaller and smaller, until some day you will find yourself a Frog." She shut her mouth to get her breath, because, you know, Frogs can only breathe a little through their skins, and then only when they are wet. Most of their air they take in through their noses and swallow with their mouths closed. That is why they cannot make long speeches. When their mouths are open they cannot swallow air.

After a while she spoke again. "It takes as many years to make a newly hatched Tadpole into a fully grown Frog," she said, "as there are toes on one of your hindfeet."

The First Tadpole did not know what a year was, but he felt sure from the way in which she spoke that it was a long, long time, and he was in a hurry to grow up. "I want to be a Frog sooner!" he said, crossly. "It isn't any fun at all being a Tadpole." The Green Brown Frog swam away, he was becoming so disagreeable.

The First Tadpole became crosser and crosser, and was very unreasonable. He did not think of the pleasant things which happened every day, but only of the trying ones. He did not know that Frogs often wished themselves Tadpoles again, and he sulked around in the pondweed all day. Every time he looked at one of his hindfeet it reminded him of what the Green Brown Frog had said, and he even grew out of patience with his tail--the same strong wiggly little tail of which he had been so proud.

"Horrid old thing!" he said, giving it a jerk. "Won't I be glad to get rid of you?" Then he thought of something--foolish, vain little First Tadpole that he was. He thought and he thought and he thought and he thought, and when his playmates swam around him he wouldn't chase them, and when they asked him what was the matter, he just answered, "Oh nothing!" as carelessly as could be.

The truth was that he wanted to be a Frog right away, and he thought he knew how he could be. He didn't want to tell the other Tadpoles because he didn't want any one else to become a Frog as soon as he. After a while he swam off to see the Snapping Turtle. He was very much afraid of the Snapping Turtle, and yet he thought him the best one to see just now. "I came to see if you would snap off my tail," said he.

"Your what?" said the Snapping Turtle, in his most surprised way.

"My tail," answered the First Tadpole, who had never had a tail snapped off, and thought it could be easily done. "I want to be a Frog to-day and not wait."

"Certainly," said the Snapping Turtle. "With pleasure! No trouble at all! Anything else I can do for you?"

"No, thank you," said the First Tadpole, "only you won't snap off too much, will you?"

"Not a bit," answered the Snapping Turtle, with a queer look in his eyes. "And if any of your friends are in a hurry to grow up, I shall be glad to help them." Then he swam toward the First Tadpole and did as he had been asked to do.

The next morning all the other Tadpoles crowded around to look at the First Tadpole. "Why-ee!" they cried. "Where is your tail?"

"I don't know," he answered, "but I think the Snapping Turtle could tell you."

"What is this?" asked the Green Brown Frog, swimming up to them. "Did the Snapping Turtle try to catch you? You poor little fellow! How did it happen?" She was very fond of the First Tadpole, and had about decided that he must be one of her sons.

"Well," he said slowly, for he didn't want the other Tadpoles to do the same thing, "I met him last evening and he--"

"Snapped at you!" exclaimed the Green Brown Frog. "It is lucky for you that he doesn't believe in eating hearty suppers, that is all I have to say! But you are a very foolish Tadpole not to keep out of his way, as you have always been told you must."

Then the First Tadpole lost his temper. "I'm not foolish, and I'm not a Tadpole," he said. "I asked him to snap it off, and now I am a Frog!"

"Oho!" said the voice of the Yellow Brown Frog behind him. "You are a Frog, are you? Let's hear you croak then. Come out on the bank and have a hopping match with me."

"I--I don't croak yet," stammered the First Tadpole, "a--and I don't care to hop."

"You are just a tailless Tadpole," said the Yellow Brown Frog sternly. "Don't any more of you youngsters try such a plan, or some of you will be Tadpole-less tails and a good many of you won't be anything."

The old Snapping Turtle waited all morning for some more Tadpoles who wanted to be made into Frogs, but none came. The Biggest Frog croaked hoarsely when he heard of it. "Tails! Tails! Tails! Tails! Tails! Tails! Tails! Tails!" said he. "That youngster will never be a strong Frog. Tadpoles must be Tadpoles, tails and all, for a long time, if they hope to ever be really fine Frogs like me." And that is so, as any Frog will tell you.

The Green Brown Frog sighed as she crawled out on the bank. "What a silly Tadpole," she said; "I'm glad he isn't my child!"

THE RUNAWAY WATER SPIDERS

When the little Water Spiders first opened their eyes, and this was as soon as they were hatched, they found themselves in a cosy home of one room which their mother had built under the water. This room had no window and only one door. There was no floor at all. When Father Stickleback had asked Mrs. Spider why she did not make a floor, she had looked at him in great surprise and said, "Why, if I had built one, I should have no place to go in and out." She really thought him quite stupid not to think of that. It often happens, you know, that really clever people think each other stupid, just because they live in different ways. Afterward, Mrs. Water Spider saw Father Stickleback's nest, and understood why he asked that question.

When her home was done, it was half as large as a big acorn and a charming place for Water Spider babies. The side walls and the rounding ceiling were all of the finest Spider silk, and the bottom was just one round doorway. The house was built under the water and fastened down by tiny ropes of Spider silk which were tied to the stems of pond plants. Mrs. Water Spider looked at it with a happy smile. "Next I must fill it with air," said she, "and then it will be ready. I am out of breath now."

She crept up the stem of the nearest plant and sat in the air for a few minutes, eating her lunch and resting. Next she walked down the stem until just the end of her body was in the air. She stood so, with her head down, then gave a little jerk and dove to her home. As she jerked, she crossed her hindlegs and caught a small bubble of air between them and her body. When she reached her home, she went quickly in the open doorway and let go of her bubble. It did not fall downward to the floor, as bubbles do in most houses, and there were two reasons for this. In the first place, there was no floor. In the second place, air always falls upward in the water. This fell up until it reached the rounded ceiling and had to stop. Just as it fell, a drop of water went out through the open doorway. The home had been full of water, you know, but now that Mrs. Spider had begun to bring in air something had to be moved to make a place for it.

She brought down thirteen more bubbles of air and then the house was filled with it. On the lower side of the open doorway there was water and on the upper side was air, and each stayed where it should. When Mrs. Spider came into her house, she always had some air caught in the hairs which covered her body, even when she did not bring a bubble of it in her hindlegs. She had to have plenty of it in her home to keep her from drowning, for she could not breathe water like a fish. "Side doors may be all right for Sticklebacks," said she, "for they do not need air, but I must have bottom doors, and I will have them too!"

After she had laid her eggs, she had some days in which to rest and visit with the Water-Boatmen who lived near. They were great friends. Belostoma used to ask the Water-Boatmen, who were his cousins, why they were so neighborly with the Water Spiders. "I don't like to see you so much with eight-legged people," he said. "They are not our kind." Belostoma was very proud of his family.

"We know that they have rather too many legs to look well," said Mrs. Water-Boatman, "but they are pleasant, and we are interested in the same things. You know we both carry air about with us in the water, and so few of our neighbors seem to care anything for it." She was a sensible little person and knew that people who are really fond of their friends do not care how many legs they have. She carried her air under her wings, but there were other Water-Boatmen, near relatives, who spread theirs over their whole bodies, and looked very silvery and beautiful when they were under water.

One day, when Mrs. Water Spider was sitting on a lily-pad and talking with her friends, a Water-Boatman rose quickly from the bottom of the pond. As soon as he got right side up (and that means as soon as he got to floating on his back), he said to her, "I heard queer sounds in your house; I was feeding near there, and the noise startled me so that I let go of the stone I was holding to, and came up. I think your eggs must be hatching."

"Really?" exclaimed Mrs. Water Spider. "I shall be so glad! A house always seems lonely to me without children." She dove to her house, and found some very fine Water Spider babies there. You may be sure she did not have much time for visiting after that. She had to hunt food and carry it down to her children, and when they were restless and impatient she stayed with them and told them stories of the great world.

Sometimes they teased to go out with her, but this she never allowed. "Wait until you are older," she would say. "It will not be so very long before you can go safely." The children thought it had been a long, long time already, and one of them made a face when his mother said this. She did not see him, and it was well for him that she did not. He should have been very much ashamed of himself for doing it.

The next time Mrs. Water Spider went for food, one of the children said, "I tell you what let's do! Let's all go down to the doorway and peek out." They looked at each other and wondered if they dared. That was something their mother had forbidden them to do. There was no window to look through and they wanted very much to see the world. At last the little fellow who had made a face said, "I'm going to, anyway." After that, his brothers and sisters went, too. And this shows how, if good little Spiders listen to naughty little Spiders, they become naughty little Spiders themselves.

All the children ran down and peeked around the edge of the door, but they couldn't see much besides water, and they had seen that before. They were sadly disappointed. Somebody said, "I'm going to put two of my legs out!" Somebody else said, "I'll put four out!" A big brother said, "I'm going to put six out!" And then another brother said "I'll put eight out! Dare you to!"

You know what naughty little Spiders would be likely to do then. Well, they did it. And, as it happened, they had just pulled their last legs through the open doorway when a Stickleback Father came along. "Aren't you rather young to be out of the nest?" said he, in his most pleasant voice.

Poor little Water Spiders! They didn't know he was one of their mother's friends, and he seemed so big to them, and the bones on his cheeks made him look so queer, and the stickles on his back were so sharp, that every one of them was afraid and let go of the wall of the house--and then!

Every one of them rose quickly to the top, into the light and the open air. They crawled upon a lily-pad and clung there, frightened, and feeling weak in all their knees. The Dragon Flies flew over them, the Wild Ducks swam past them, and on a log not far away they saw a long row of Mud Turtles sunning themselves. Why nothing dreadful happened, one cannot tell. Perhaps it was bad enough as it was, for they were so scared that they could only huddle close together and cry, "We want our mother."

Here Mrs. Water Spider found them. She came home with something for dinner, and saw her house empty. Of course she knew where to look, for, as she said, "If they stepped outside the door, they would be quite sure to tumble up into the air." She took them home, one at a time, and how she ever did it nobody knows.

When they were all safely there and had eaten the food that was waiting for them, Mrs. Spider, who had not scolded them at all, said, "Look me straight in the eye, every one of you! Will you promise never to run away again?"

Instead of saying at once, "Yes, mother," as they should have done, one of them answered, "Why, we didn't run away. We were just peeking around the edge of the doorway, and we got too far out, and somebody came along and scared us so that we let go, and then we couldn't help falling up into the air."

"Oh, no," said their mother, "you couldn't help it then, of course. But who told you that you might peep out of the door?"

The little Water Spiders hung their heads and looked very much ashamed. Their mother went on, "You needn't say that you were not to blame. You were to blame, and you began to run away as soon as you took the first step toward the door, only you didn't know that you were going so far. Tell me," she said, "whether you would ever have gone to the top of the water if you had not taken that first step?"

The little Water Spiders were more ashamed than ever, but they had to look her in the eye and promise to be good.

It is very certain that not one of those children even peeped around the edge of the doorway from that day until their mother told them that they might go into the world and build houses for themselves. "Remember just one thing," she said, as they started away. "Always take your food home to eat." And they always did, for no Water Spider who has been well brought up will ever eat away from his own home.

THE SLOW LITTLE MUD TURTLE

When the twenty little Mud Turtles broke their egg-shells one hot summer day, and poked their way up through the warm sand in which they had been buried, they looked almost as much alike as so many raindrops. The Mother Turtle who was sunning herself on the bank near by, said to her friends, "Why! There are my children! Did you ever see a finer family? I believe I will go over and speak to them."

Most of the young Mud Turtles crawled quickly out of the sand and broken shells, and began drying themselves in the sunshine. One slow little fellow stopped to look at the broken shells, stubbed one of his front toes on a large piece and then sat down until it should stop aching. "Wait for me!" he called out to his brothers and sisters. "I'm coming in a minute."

The other little Turtles waited, but when his toe was comfortable again and he started toward them, he met a very interesting Snail and talked a while with him. "Come on," said the Biggest Little Turtle. "Don't let's wait any longer. He can catch up."

So they sprawled along until they came to a place where they could sit in a row on an old log, and they climbed onto it and sat just close enough together and not at all too close. Then the Slow Little Turtle came hurrying over the sand with a rather cross look in his eyes and putting his feet down a little harder than he needed to--quite as though he were out of patience about something. "Why didn't you Turtles wait for me?" he grumbled. "I was coming right along."

[Illustration: "GOOD MORNING," SAID SHE. "I BELIEVE YOU ARE MY CHILDREN?" Page 85]

Just then the Mother Turtle came up. "Good morning," said she. "I believe you are my children?"

The little Mud Turtles looked at each other and didn't say a word. This was not because they were rude or bashful, but because they did not know what to say. And that, you know, was quite right, for unless one has something worth saying, it is far better to say nothing at all.

She drew a long Mud Turtle breath and answered her own question. "Yes," she said, "you certainly are, for I saw you scrambling out of the sand a little while ago, and you came from the very place where I laid my eggs and covered them during the first really warm nights this year. I was telling your father only yesterday that it was about time for you to hatch. The sun has been so hot lately that I was sure you would do well."

The Mother Turtle stretched her head this way and that until there was hardly a wrinkle left in her neck-skin, she was so eager to see them all. "Why are you not up here with your brothers and sisters?" she asked suddenly of the Slow Little Turtle, who was trying to make a place for himself on the log.

"They didn't wait for me," he said. "I was coming right along but they wouldn't wait. I think they are just as mea----"

The Mother Turtle raised one of her forefeet until all five of its toes with their strong claws were pointing at him. She also raised her head as far as her upper shell would let her. "So you are the one," she said. "I thought you were when I heard you trying to make the others wait. It is too bad."

She looked so stern that the Slow Little Turtle didn't dare finish what he had begun to say, yet down in his little Turtle heart he thought, "Now they are going to catch it!" He was sure his mother was going to scold the other Turtle children for leaving him. He wanted to see what they would do, so he looked out of his right eye at the ten brothers and sisters on that side, and out of his left eye at the nine brothers and sisters on that side. He could do this very easily, because his eyes were not on the front of his head like those of some people, but one on each side.

"I have raised families of young Turtles every year," said the Mother Turtle. "The first year I had only a few children, the next year I had more, and so it has gone--every year a few more children than the year before--until now I never know quite how many I do have. But there is always one Slow Little Turtle who lags behind and wants the others to wait for him. That makes him miss his share of good things, and then he is quite certain to be cross and think it is somebody else's fault."

The Slow Little Turtle felt the ten brothers and sisters on his right side looking at him out of their left eyes, and the nine brothers and sisters on his left side looking at him out of their right eyes. He drew in his head and his tail and his legs, until all they could see was his rounded upper shell, his shell side-walls, and the yellow edge of his flat lower shell. He would have liked to draw them in too, but of course he couldn't do that.

"I did hope," said the Mother Turtle, "that I might have one family without such a child in it. I cannot help loving even a slow child who is cross, if he is hatched from one of my eggs, yet it makes me sad--very, very sad."

"Try to get over this," she said to the Slow Little Turtle, "before it is too late. And you," she added, turning to his brothers and sisters, "must be patient with him. We shall not have him with us long."

"What do you mean?" asked the Slow Little Turtle, peeping out from between his shells. "I'm not going away."

"You do not want to," said his mother, "but you will not be with us long unless you learn to keep up with the rest. Something always happens to pond people who are too slow. I cannot tell you what it will be, yet it is sure to be something. I remember so well my first slow child--and how he--" She began to cry, and since she could not easily get her forefeet to her eyes, she sprawled to the pond and swam off with only her head and a little of her upper shell showing above the water.

The Slow Little Turtle was really frightened by what his mother had said, and for a few days he tried to keep up with the others. Nothing happened to him, and so he grew careless and made people wait for him just because he was not quite ready to go with them, or because he wanted to do this or look at that or talk to some other person. He was a very trying little Turtle, yet his mother loved him and did not like it when the rest called him a Land Tortoise. It is all right, you know, to be a Land Tortoise when your father and mother are Land Tortoises, and these cousins of the Turtles look so much like them that some people cannot tell them apart. That is because they forget that the Tortoises live on land, have higher back shells, and move very, very slowly. Turtles live more in the water and can move quickly if they will. This is why other Turtles sometimes make fun of a slow brother by calling him a Land Tortoise.

One beautiful sunshiny afternoon, when most of the twenty little Turtles were sitting on a floating log by the edge of the pond, their mother was with some of her friends on another log near by. She looked often at her children, and thought how handsome their rounded-up back shells were in the sunshine with the little red and yellow markings showing on the black. She could see their strong little pointed tails too, and their webbed feet with a stout claw on each toe. She was so proud that she could not help talking about them. "Is there any sight more beautiful," she said, "than a row of good little Turtles?"

"Yes," said a fine old fellow who was floating near her, "a row of their mothers!" He was a Turtle whom she had never liked very well, but now she began to think that he was rather agreeable after all. She was just noticing how beautifully the skin wrinkled on his neck, when she heard a splash and saw two terrible great two-legged animals wading into the pond from the shore.

"Boys!" she cried, "Boys!" And she sprawled off the end of her log and slid into the water, all her friends following her. The Biggest Little Turtle saw these great animals coming toward him. He sprawled off the end of his log and slid into the water, and all his brothers and sisters followed him except the Slow Little Turtle. "Wait for me," he said. "I'm coming in just a----"

Then one of these great animals stooped over and picked him up, and held him bottom side uppermost and rapped on that side, which was flat; and on the other side, which was rounded; and stared at him with two great eyes. Next the other great animal took him and turned him over and rapped on his shells and stared at him. The poor Slow Little Turtle drew in his head and tail and legs and kept very, very still. He wished that he had side-pieces of shell all around now, instead of just one on each side between his legs. He was thinking over and over, "Something has happened! Something has happened!" And he knew that back in the pond his mother would be trying to find him and could not.

The boys carried him to the edge of the meadow and put him down on the grass. He lay perfectly still for a long, long time, and when he thought they had forgotten about him he tried to run away. Then they laughed and picked him up again, and one of them took something sharp and shiny and cut marks into his upper shell. This did not really give him pain, yet, as he said afterward, "It hurts almost as much to think you are going to be hurt, as it does to be hurt."

It was not until the sun went down that the boys let the Slow Little Turtle go. Then he was very, very tired, but he wanted so much to get back to his home in the pond that he started at once by moonlight. This was the first time he had ever seen the moon, for, except when they are laying eggs, Turtles usually sleep at night. He was not quite sure which way he should go, and if it had not been for the kindness of the Tree Frog he might never have seen his brothers and sisters again. You know the Tree Frog had been carried away when he was young, before he came to live with the meadow people, so he knew how to be sorry for the Slow Little Turtle.

The Tree Frog hopped along ahead to show the way, and the Turtle followed until they reached a place from which they could see the pond. "Good night!" said the Tree Frog. "You can find your way now."

"Good night!" said the Turtle. "I wish I might help you some time."

"Never mind me," said the Tree Frog. "Help somebody else and it will be all right." He hopped back toward his home, and for a long time afterward the Turtle heard his cheerful "Pukr-r-rup! Pukr-r-rup!" sounding over the dewy grass and through the still air. At the edge of the pond the Slow Little Turtle found his nineteen brothers and sisters sound asleep. "I'm here!" he cried joyfully, poking first one and then another of them with his head.

The Biggest Little Turtle moved without awakening. "I tell you I'm not hungry," he murmured. "I don't want to get up." And again he fell fast asleep.

So the Slow Little Turtle did not disturb him, but cuddled inside his two shells and went to sleep also. He was so tired that he did not awaken until the sun was high in the sky. When he did open his eyes, his relatives were sitting around looking at him, and he remembered all that had happened before he slept. "Does my shell look very bad?" he cried. "I wish I could see it. Oh, I am so glad to get back! I'll never be slow again, Never! Never!"

His mother came and leaned her shell lovingly against his. "If you will only learn to keep up with your brothers and sisters," she said "I shall not be sorry that the boys carried you off."

"You just wait and see," said the Slow Little Turtle. And he was as good as his word. After that he was always the first to slip from the log to the water if anything scared them; and when, one day, a strange Turtle from another pond came to visit, he said to the Turtles who had always lived there, "Why do you call that young fellow with the marked shell 'The Slow Little Turtle?' He is the quickest one in his family."

The pond people looked at each other and laughed. "That is queer!" they said. "After this we will call him 'The Quick Little Turtle.'"

This made him very happy, and when, once in a while, somebody forgot and by mistake called him "The Quick Slow Little Turtle," he said he rather liked it because it showed that a Turtle needn't keep his faults if he did have them.

THE DRAGON-FLY CHILDREN AND THE SNAPPING TURTLE

The Dragon-Flies have always lived near the pond. Not the same ones that are there now, of course, but the great-great-great-grandfathers of these. A person would think that, after a family had lived so long in a place, all the neighbors would be fond of them, yet it is not so. The Dragon-Flies may be very good people--and even the Snapping Turtle says that they are--still, they are so peculiar that many of their neighbors do not like them at all. Even when they are only larvae, or babies, they are not good playmates, for they have such a bad habit of putting everything into their mouths. Indeed, the Stickleback Father once told the little Sticklebacks that they should not stir out of the nest, unless they would promise to keep away from the young Dragon-Flies.

The Stickleback Mothers said that it was all the fault of the Dragon-Fly Mothers. "What can you expect," exclaimed one of them, "when Dragon-Fly eggs are so carelessly laid? I saw a Dragon-Fly Mother laying some only yesterday, and how do you suppose she did it? Just flew around in the sunshine and visited with her friends, and once in a while flew low enough to touch the water and drop one in. It is disgraceful!"

The Minnow Mothers did not think it was so much in the way the eggs were laid, "although," said one, "I always lay mine close together, instead of scattering them over the whole pond." They thought the trouble came from bad bringing up or no bringing up at all. Each egg, you know, when it is laid, drops to the bottom of the pond, and the children are hatched and grow up there, and do not even see their fathers and mothers.

Now most of the larvae were turning into Nymphs, which are half-grown Dragon Flies. They had been short and plump, and now they were longer and more slender, and there were little bunches on their shoulders where the wings were growing under their skin. They had outgrown their old skins a great many times, and had to wriggle out of them to be at all comfortable. When a Dragon-Fly child became too big for his skin, he hooked the two sharp claws of each of his six feet firmly into something, unfastened his skin down the back, and wriggled out, leaving it to roll around in the water until it became just part of the mud.

Like most growing children, the Dragon-Fly larvae and Nymphs had to eat a great deal. Their stomachs were as long as their bodies, and they were never really happy unless their stomachs were full. They always ate plain food and plenty of it, and they never ate between meals. They had breakfast from the time they awakened in the morning until the sun was high in the sky, then they had dinner until the sun was low in the sky, and supper from that time until it grew dark and they went to sleep: but never a mouthful between meals, no matter how hungry they might be. They said this was their only rule about eating, and they would keep it.

They were always slow children. You would think that, with six legs apiece and three joints in each leg, they might walk quite fast, yet they never did. When they had to, they hurried in another way by taking a long leap through the water. Of course they breathed water like their neighbors, the fishes and the Tadpoles. They did not breathe it into their mouths, or through gills, but took it in through some openings in the back part of their bodies. When they wanted to hurry, they breathed this water out so suddenly that it sent them quickly ahead.

The Snapping Turtle had called them "bothering bugs" one day when he was cross (and that was the day after he had been cross, and just before the day when he was going to be cross again), and they didn't like him and wanted to get even. They all put their queer little three-cornered heads together, and there was an ugly look in their great staring eyes.

"Horrid old thing!" said one larva. "I wish I could sting him."

"Well, you can't," said a Nymph, turning towards him so suddenly that he leaped. "You haven't any sting, and you never will have, so you just keep still." It was not at all nice in her to speak that way, but she was not well brought up, you know, and that, perhaps, is a reason why one should excuse her for talking so to her little brother. She was often impatient, and said she could never go anywhere without one of the larvae tagging along.

"I tell you what let's do," said another Nymph. "Let's all go together to the shallow water where he suns himself, and let's all stand close to each other, and then, when he comes along, let's stick out our lips at him!"

"Both lips?" asked the larvae.

"Well, our lower lips anyway," answered the Nymph. "Our upper lips are so small they don't matter."

"We'll do it," exclaimed all the Dragon-Fly children, and they started together to walk on the pond-bottom to the shallow water. They thought it would scare the Snapping Turtle dreadfully. They knew that whenever they stuck out their lower lips at the small fishes and bugs, they swam away as fast as they could. The Giant Water-Bug (Belostoma), was the only bug who was not afraid of them when they made faces. Indeed, the lower lip of a Dragon-Fly child might well frighten people, for it is fastened on a long, jointed, arm-like thing, and has pincers on it with which it catches and holds its food. Most of the time, the Dragon-Fly child keeps the joint bent, and so holds his lip up to his face like a mask. But sometimes he straightens the joint and holds his lip out before him, and then its pincers catch hold of things. He does this when he is hungry.

When they reached the shallow water, the Dragon-Fly children stood close together, with the larvae in the middle and the Nymphs all around them. The Snapping Turtle was nowhere to be seen, so they had to wait. "Aren't you scared?" whispered one larva to another.

"Scared? Dah! Who's afraid," answered he.

"Oh, look!" cried a Nymph. "There go some grown-up Dragon-Flies over our heads. Just you wait until I change my skin once more, and then won't I have a good time! I'll dry my wings and then I'll----"

"Sh-h!" said one of the larvae. "Here comes the Snapping Turtle."

Sure enough, there he came through the shallow water, his wet back-shell partly out of it and shining in the sunlight. He came straight toward the Dragon-Fly children, and they were glad to see that he did not look hungry. They thought he might be going to take a nap after his dinner. Then they all stood even closer together and stuck out their lower lips at him. They thought he might run away when they did this. They felt sure that he would at least be very badly frightened.

The Snapping Turtle did not seem to see them at all. It was queer. He just waddled on and on, coming straight toward them. "Ah-h-h!" said he. "How sleepy I do feel! I will lie down in the sunshine and rest." He took a few more steps, which brought his great body right over the crowd of Dragon-Fly children. "I think I will draw in my head," said he (the Dragon-Fly children looked at each other), "and my tail (here two of the youngest larvae began to cry) and lie down." He began to draw in his legs very, very slowly, and just as his great hard lower shell touched the mud, the last larva crawled out under his tail. The Nymphs had already gotten away.

"Oh," said the Dragon-Fly children to each other, "Wasn't it awful!"

"Humph," said the Snapping Turtle, talking to himself--he had gotten into the way of doing that because he had so few friends--"How dreadfully they did scare me!" Then he laughed a grim Snapping Turtle laugh, and went to sleep.

THE SNAPPY SNAPPING TURTLE

There was but one Snapping Turtle in the pond, and he was the only person there who had ever been heard to wish for another. He had not always lived there, and could just remember leaving his brothers and sisters when he was young. "I was carried away from my people," he said, "and kept on land for a few days. Then I was brought here and have made it my home ever since."

One could tell by looking at him that he was related to the Mud Turtles. He had upper and lower shells like them, and could draw in his head and legs and tail when he wanted to. His shells were gray, quite the color of a clay-bank, and his head was larger than those of the Mud Turtles. His tail was long and scaly and pointed, and his forelegs were large and warty. There were fine, strong webs between his toes, as there were between the toes of his relatives, the Mud Turtles.

When he first came to live in the pond, people were sorry for him, and tried to make him feel at home. He had a chance to win many friends and have all his neighbors fond of him, but he was too snappy. When the water was just warm enough, and his stomach was full, and he had slept well the night before, and everything was exactly as he wished it to be,--ah, then he was a very agreeable Turtle, and was ready to talk in the most gracious way to his neighbors. That was all very well. Anybody can be good-natured when everything is exactly right and he can have his own way. But the really delightful people, you know, are the ones who are pleasant when things go wrong.

It was a Mud Turtle Father who first spoke to him. "I hope you'll like the pond," said he. "We think it very homelike and comfortable."

"Humph! Shallow little hole!" snapped the one who had just come. "I bump my head on the bottom every time I dive."

"That is too bad," exclaimed the Mud Turtle Father. "I hope you dive where there is a soft bottom."

"Sometimes I do and sometimes I don't," answered the Snapping Turtle. "I can't bother to swim down slowly and try it, and then go back to dive. When I want to dive, I want to dive, and that's all there is to it."

"Yes," said the Mud Turtle Father. "I know how it is when one has the diving feeling. I hope your head will not trouble you much, and that you will soon be used to our waters." He spread his toes and swam strongly away, pushing against the water with his webbed feet.

"Humph!" said the Snapping Turtle to himself. "It is all very well to talk about getting used to these waters, but I never shall. I can hardly see now for the pain in the right side of my head, where I bumped it. Or was it the left side I hit? Queer I can't remember!" Then he swam to shallow water, and drew himself into his shell, and lay there and thought how badly he felt, and how horrid the pond was, and what poor company his neighbors were, and what a disagreeable world this is for Snapping Turtles.

The Mud Turtle Father went home and told his wife all about it. "What a disagreeable fellow!" she said. "But then, he is a bachelor, and bachelors are often queer."

"I never was," said her husband.

"Oh!" said she. And, being a wise wife, she did not say anything else. She knew, however, that Mr. Mud Turtle was a much more agreeable fellow since he had married and learned to think more of somebody else than of himself. It is the people who think too much of themselves you know, who are most unhappy in this world.

The Eels also tried to be friendly, and, when he dove to the bottom, called to him to stay and visit with them. "You must excuse us from making the first call," they said. "We go out so little in the daytime."

"Humph!" said the Snapping Turtle. "Do you good to get away from home more. No wonder your eyes are weak, when you lie around in the mud of the dark pond-bottom all day. Indeed, I'll not stay. You can come to see me like other people."

Then he swam away and told the Clams what he had said, and he acted quite proud of what was really dreadful rudeness. "It'll do them good to hear the truth," said he. "I always speak right out. They are as bad as the Water-Adder. They have no backbone."

The Clams listened politely and said nothing. They never did talk much. The Snapping Turtle was mistaken though, when he said that the Eels and the Water-Adder had no backbone. They really had much more than he, but they wore theirs inside, while his was spread out in the shape of a shell for everybody to see.

He did not even try to keep his temper. He became angry one day because Belostoma, the Giant Water-Bug, ate something which he wanted for himself. His eyes glared and his horny jaws snapped, and he waved his long, pointed, scaly tail in a way which was terrible to see. "You are a good-for-nothing bug," he said. "You do no work, and you eat more than any other person of your size here. Nobody likes you, and there isn't a little fish in the pond who would be seen with you if he could help it. They all hide if they see you coming. I'll be heartily glad when you get your wings and fly away. Don't let any of your friends lay their eggs in this pond. I've seen enough of your family."

Of course this made Belostoma feel very badly. He was not a popular bug, and it is possible that if he could have had his own way, he would have chosen to be a Crayfish or a Stickleback, rather than what he was. As for his not working--there was nothing for him to do, so how could he work? He had to eat, or he would not grow, and since the Snapping Turtle was a hearty eater himself, he should have had the sense to keep still about that. Belostoma told the Mud Turtles what the Snapping Turtle had said, and the Mud Turtle Father spoke of it to the Snapping Turtle.

By that time the Snapping Turtle was feeling better natured and was very gracious. "Belostoma shouldn't remember those things," said he, moving one warty foreleg. "When I am angry, I often say things that I do not mean; but then, I get right over it. I had almost forgotten my little talk with him. I don't see any reason for telling him I am sorry. He is very silly to think so much of it." He lifted his big head quite high, and acted as though it was really a noble thing to be ugly and then forget about it. He might just as sensibly ask people to admire him for not eating when his stomach was full, or for lying still when he was too tired to swim.

When the Mud Turtle Mother heard of this, she was quite out of patience. "All he cares for," said she, "is just Snapping Turtle, Snapping Turtle, Snapping Turtle. When he is good-natured, he thinks everybody else ought to be; and when he is bad-tempered he doesn't care how other people feel. He will never be any more agreeable until he does something kind for somebody, and I don't see any chance of that happening."

There came a day, though, when the pond people were glad that the Snapping Turtle lived there. Two boys were wading in the edge of the pond, splashing the water and scaring all the people who were near them. The Sticklebacks turned pale all over, as they do when they are badly frightened. The Yellow Brown Frog was so scared that he emptied out the water he had saved for wetting his skin in dry weather. He had a great pocket in his body filled with water, for if his skin should get dry he couldn't breathe through it, and unless he carried water with him he could not stay ashore at all.

The boys had even turned the Mud Turtle Father onto his back in the sunshine, where he lay, waving his feet in the air, but not strong enough to get right side up again. The Snapping Turtle was taking a nap in deep water, when the frightened fishes came swimming toward him as fast as their tails would take them. "What is the matter?" said he.

"Boys!" cried they. "Boys! The dreadful, splashing, Turtle-turning kind."

"Humph!" said the Snapping Turtle. "I'll have to see about that. How many are there?"

"Two!" cried the Sticklebacks and Minnows together.

"And there is only one of me," said the Snapping Turtle to himself. "I must have somebody to help me. Oh, Belostoma," he cried, as the Giant Water-Bug swam past. "Help me drive those boys away."

"With pleasure," said Belostoma, who liked nothing better than this kind of work. Off they started for the place where the boys were wading. The Snapping Turtle took long, strong strokes with his webbed feet, and Belostoma could not keep up with him. The Snapping Turtle saw this. "Jump onto my back," cried he. "You are a light fellow. Hang tight."

Belostoma jumped onto the Snapping Turtle's clay-colored shell, and when he found himself slipping off the back end of it, he stuck his claws into the Snapping Turtle's tail and held on in that way. He knew that he was not easily hurt, even if he did make a fuss when he bumped his head. As soon as they got near the boys, the Snapping Turtle spoke over his back-shell to Belostoma. "Slide off now," said he, "and drive away the smaller boy. Don't stop to talk with these Bloodsuckers."

So Belostoma slid off and swam toward the smaller boy, and he ran out his stout little sucking tube and stung him on the leg. Just then the Snapping Turtle brought his horny jaws together on one of the larger boy's feet. There was a great splashing and dashing as the boys ran to the shore, and three Bloodsuckers, who had fastened themselves to the boy's legs, did not have time to drop off, and were carried ashore and never seen again.

[Illustration: THERE WAS A GREAT SPLASHING AND DASHING. Page 117]

"There!" said the Snapping Turtle. "That's done. I don't know what the pond people would do, if you and I were not here to look after them, Belostoma."

"I'm glad I happened along," said the Giant Water-Bug quietly, "but you will have to do it all after this. I'm about ready to leave the pond. I think I'll go to-morrow."

"Going to-morrow!" exclaimed the Snapping Turtle. "I'm sorry. Of course I know you can never come back, but send your friends here to lay their eggs.

We mustn't be left without some of your family."

"Thank you," said Belostoma, and he did not show that he remembered some quite different things which the Snapping Turtle had said before, about his leaving the pond. And that showed that he was a very wise bug as well as a brave one.

"Humph!" said the Snapping Turtle. "There is the Mud Turtle Father on his back." And he ran to him and pushed him over onto his feet. "Oh, thank you," cried the Mud Turtle Mother. "I was not strong enough to do that."

"Always glad to help my neighbors," said the Snapping Turtle. "Pleasant day, isn't it? I must tell the fishes that the boys are gone. The poor little fellows were almost too scared to swim." And he went away with a really happy look on his face.

"There!" said the Mud Turtle Mother to her husband. "He has begun to help people, and now he likes them, and is contented, I always told you so!"

THE CLEVER WATER-ADDER

None of the pond people were alone more than the Water-Adders. The Snapping Turtle was left to himself a great deal until the day when he and Belostoma drove away the boys. After that his neighbors began to understand him better and he was less grumpy, so that those who wore shells were soon quite fond of him.

Belostoma did not have many friends among the smaller people, and only a few among the larger ones. They said that he was cruel, and that he had a bad habit of using his stout sucking tube to sting with. Still, Belostoma did not care; he said, "A Giant Water-Bug does not always live in the water. I shall have my wings soon, and leave the water and marry. After that, I shall fly away on my wedding trip. Mrs. Belostoma may go with me, if she feels like doing so after laying her eggs here. I shall go anyway. And I shall flutter and sprawl around the light, and sting people who bother me, and have a happy time." That was Belostoma's way. He would sting people who bothered him, but then he always said that they need not have bothered him. And perhaps that was so.

With the Water-Adders it was different. They were good-natured enough, yet the Mud Turtles and Snapping Turtle were the only ones who ever called upon them and found them at home. The small people without shells were afraid of them, and the Clams and Pond Snails never called upon any one. The Minnows said they could not bear the looks of the Adders--they had such ugly mouths and such quick motions. The larger fishes kept away on account of their children, who were small and tender.

One might think that the Sand-Hill Cranes, the Fish Hawks, and the other shore families would have been good friends for them, but when they called, the Adders were always away. People said that the Adders were afraid of them.

The Yellow Brown Frog wished that the Adders could be scared, badly scared, some time: so scared that a chilly feeling would run down their backs from their heads clear to the tips of their tails. "I wish," said he, "that the chilly feeling would be big enough to go way through to their bellies. Their bellies are only the front side of their backs, anyway," he added, "because they are so thin." Of course this was a dreadful wish to make, but people said that one of the Adders had frightened the Yellow Brown Frog so that he never got over it, and this was the reason he felt so.

The Water-Adders were certainly the cleverest people in the pond, and there was one Mother Adder who was so very bright that they called her "the Clever Water-Adder." She could do almost anything, and she knew it. She talked about it, too, and that showed bad taste, and was one reason why she was not liked better. She could swim very fast, could creep, glide, catch hold of things with her tail, hang herself from the branch of a tree, lift her head far into the air, leap, dart, bound, and dive. All her family could do these things, but she could do them a little the best.

One day she was hanging over the pond in a very graceful position, with her tail twisted carelessly around a willow branch. The Snapping Turtle and a Mud Turtle Father were in the shallow water below her. Her slender forked tongue was darting in and out of her open mouth. She was using her tongue in this way most of the time. "It is useful in feeling of things," she said, "and then, I have always thought it quite becoming." She could see herself reflected in the still water below her, and she noticed how prettily the dark brown of her back shaded into the white of her belly. You see she was vain as well as clever.

The Snapping Turtle felt cross to-day, and had come to see if a talk with her would not make him feel better. The Mud Turtle was tired of having the children sprawl around him, and of Mrs. Mud Turtle telling about the trouble she had to get the right kind of food.

The Clever Water-Adder spoke first of the weather. "It must be dreadfully hot for the shore people," she said. "Think of their having to wear the same feathers all the year and fly around in the sunshine to find food for their children."

"Ah yes," said the Mud Turtle. "How they must wish for shells!"

"Humph!" said the Snapping Turtle. "What for? To fly with? Let them come in swimming with their children, if they are warm and tired."

The Water-Adder laughed in her snaky way, and showed her sharp teeth. "I have heard," she said, "that when the Wild Ducks bring their children here to swim, they do not always take so many home as they brought."

The Snapping Turtle became very much interested in his warty right foreleg, and did not seem to hear what she said. The Mud Turtle smiled. "I have heard," she went on, "that when young Ducks dive head first, they are quite sure to come up again, but that when they dive feet first, they never come up."

"What do you mean?" asked the Snapping Turtle, and he was snappy about it.

"Oh, nothing," replied the Water-Adder, swinging her head back and forth and looking at the scales on her body.

"I know what you mean," said the Snapping Turtle, "and you know what you mean, but I have to eat something, and if I am swimming under the water and a Duckling paddles along just above me and sticks his foot into my mouth, I am likely to swallow him before I think."

The Water-Adder saw that he was provoked by what she had said, so she talked about something else. "I think the Ducks spoil their children," said she. "They make such a fuss over them, and they are not nearly so bright as my children. Why, mine hatch as soon as the eggs are laid, and go hunting at once. They are no trouble at all."

"I never worry about mine," said the Mud Turtle, "although their mother thinks it is not safe for them all to sleep at once, as they do on a log in the sunshine."

"It isn't," said the Adder decidedly. "I never close my eyes. None of us Adders do. Nobody can ever say that we close our eyes to danger." They couldn't shut their eyes if they wanted to, because they had no eyelids, but she did not speak of that. "How stupid people are," she said.

"Most of them," remarked the Turtles.

"All of them," she said, "except us Adders and the Turtles. I even think that some of the Turtles are a little queer, don't you?"

"We have thought so," said the Mud Turtle.

"They certainly are," agreed the Snapping Turtle, who was beginning to feel much better natured.

"What did you say?" asked the Adder who, like all her family, was a little deaf.

"Ouch!" exclaimed the Snapping Turtle. "Ouch! Ouch!"

"What is the matter?" asked the Mud Turtle. Then he began to slap the water with his short, stout tail, and say "Ouch!"

Two naughty young Water-Boatmen had swum quietly up on their backs, and stung the Turtles on their tails. Then they swam away, pushing themselves quickly through the water with swift strokes of their hairy oar-legs.

"Ah-h-h!" exclaimed the Snapping Turtle, and he backed into the mud, knowing that fine, soft mud is the best thing in the world for stings.

"Ah-h-h!" exclaimed the Mud Turtle, "if I could only reach my tail with my head, or even with one of my hind feet!"

"Reach your tail with your head?" asked the Water-Adder in her sweetest voice. "Nothing is easier." And she wound herself around the willow branch in another graceful position, and took the tip of her tail daintily between her teeth.

"Humph!" said the Snapping Turtle, and he pulled his tail out of the mud and swam away.

"Ugh!" said the Mud Turtle, and he swam away with the Snapping Turtle.

"What a rude person she is!" they said. "Always trying to show how much more clever she is than other people. We would rather be stupid and polite."

After a while the Snapping Turtle said, "But then, you know, we are not stupid."

"Of course not," replied the Mud Turtle, "not even queer."

THE GOOD LITTLE CRANES WHO WERE BAD

When the Sand-Hill Cranes were married, they began to work for a home of their own. To be sure, they had chosen a place for it beforehand, yet there were other things to think about, and some of their friends told them it would be very foolish to build on the ground. "There are so many accidents to ground nests," these friends said. "There are Snakes, you know, and Rats, and a great many other people whom you would not want to have look in on your children. Besides, something might fall on it."

The young couple talked this all over and decided to build in a tree. "We are not afraid of Snakes and Rats," they said, "but we would fear something falling on the nest." They were talking to quite an old Crane when they said this.

"Do you mean to build in a tree?" said he. "My dear young friends, don't do that. Just think, a high wind might blow the nest down and spoil everything. Do whatever you wish, but don't build in a tree." Then he flew away.

"Dear me!" exclaimed young Mrs. Crane, "one tells me to do this and never to do that. Another tells me to do that and never to do this. I shall just please myself since I cannot please my friends."

"And which place do you choose?" asked her husband, who always liked whatever she did.

"I shall build on the ground," she said decidedly. "If the tree falls, it may hit the nest and it may not, but if we build in the tree and it falls, we are sure to hit the ground."

"How wise you are!" exclaimed her husband. "I believe people get in a way of building just so, and come to think that no other way can be right." Which shows that Mr. Sand-Hill Crane was also wise.

Both worked on the nest, bringing roots and dried grasses with which to build it up. Sometimes they went to dance with their friends, and when they did they bowed most of the time to each other. They did not really care very much about going, because they were so interested in the nest. This they had to build quite high from the ground, on account of their long legs. "If I were a Duck," said Mrs. Sand-Hill Crane, "it would do very well for me to sit on the nest, but with my legs? Never! I would as soon sit on two bare branches as to have them doubled under me." So she tried the nest until it was just as high as her legs were long.

When it was high enough, she laid in it two gray eggs with brown spots. After that she did no more dancing, but stood with a leg on either side of the nest, and her soft body just over the eggs to keep them warm. It was very tiresome work, and sometimes Mr. Crane covered the eggs while she went fishing. The Cranes are always very kind to their wives.

This, you know, was the first time that either had had a nest, and it was all new and wonderful to them. They thought that there never had been such a beautiful home. They often stood on the ground beside it, and poked it this way and that with their bills, and said to each other, "Just look at this fine root that I wove in," or, "Have you noticed how well that tuft of dried grass looks where I put it?" As it came near the time for their eggs to hatch, they could hardly bear to be away long enough to find food.

One day young Mr. Sand-Hill Crane came home much excited. "Our neighbors, the Cranes who live across the pond," said he, "had two children hatched this morning."

"Oh, how glad I am!" cried his wife. "How glad I am! Those eggs were laid just before ours, which must hatch very soon now."

"That is what I thought," said he. "I feel so sorry for them, though, for I saw their children, and they are dreadfully homely,--not at all like their parents, who are quite good-looking."

"I must see them myself," said his wife, "and if you will cover the eggs while I go for food, I will just peep in on them. I will hurry back." She flew steadily across the pond, which was not very wide, and asked to see the babies. She had never seen any Crane children, you know, since she herself was little. She thought them very ugly to look at, and wondered how their mother could seem bright and cheerful with two such disappointing children. She said all the polite things that she honestly could, then got something to eat, and flew home. "They are very, very homely," she said to her husband, "and I think it queer. All their older children are good-looking."

She had hardly said this when she heard a faint tapping sound in the nest. She looked, and there was the tip of a tiny beak showing through the shell of one egg. She stood on one side of the nest, watching, and her husband stood on the other while their oldest child slowly made his way out. They dared not help for fear of hurting him, and besides, all the other Cranes had told them that they must not.

"Oh, look!" cried the young mother. "What a dear little bill!"

"Ah!" said the young father. "Did you ever see such a neck?"

"Look at those legs," cried she. "What a beautiful child he is!"

"He looks just like you," said the father, "and I am glad of it."

"Ah, no," said she. "He is exactly like you." And she began to clear away the broken egg-shell.

Soon the other Crane baby poked her bill out, and again the young parents stood around and admired their child. They could not decide which was the handsomer, but they were sure that both were remarkable babies. They felt more sorry than ever for their neighbors across the pond, who had such homely children. They took turns in covering their own damp little Cranes, and were very, very happy.

Before this, it had been easy to get what food they wanted, for there had been two to work for two. Now there were two to work for four, and that made it much harder. There was no time for dancing, and both father and mother worked steadily, yet they were happier than ever, and neither would have gone back to the careless old days for all the food in the pond or all the dances on the beach.

The little Cranes grew finely. They changed their down for pin-feathers, and then these grew into fine brownish gray feathers, like those which their parents wore. They were good children, too, and very well brought up. They ate whatever food was given to them, and never found fault with it. When they left the nest for the first time, they fluttered and tumbled and had trouble in learning to walk. A Mud Turtle Father who was near, told them that this was because their legs were too long and too few.

"Well," said the brother, as he picked himself up and tried to stand on one leg while he drew the other foot out of the tangled grass, "they may be too long, but I'm sure there are enough of them. When I'm thinking about one, I never can tell what the other will do."

Still, it was not long before they could walk and wade and even fly. Then they met the other pond people, and learned to tell a Stickleback from a Minnow. They did not have many playmates. The saucy little Kingfishers sat on branches over their heads, the Wild Ducks waddled or swam under their very bills, the Fish Hawks floated in air above them, and the Gulls screamed hoarsely to them as they circled over the pond, yet none of them were long-legged and stately. The things that the other birds enjoyed most, they could not do, and sometimes they did not like it very well. One night they were talking about the Gulls, when they should have been asleep, and their father told them to tuck their heads right under their wings and not let him hear another word from them. They did tuck their heads under their wings, but they peeped out between the feathers, and when they were sure their father and mother were asleep, they walked softly away and planned to do something naughty.

"I'm tired of being good," said the brother. "The Gulls never are good. They scream, and snatch, and contradict, and have lots of fun. Let's be bad just for fun."

"All right," said his sister. "What shall we do?"

"That's the trouble," said he. "I can't think of anything naughty that I really care for."

Each stood on one leg and thought for a while. "We might run away," said she.

"Where would we go?" asked he.

"We might go to the meadow," said she. So they started off in the moonlight and went to the meadow, but all the people there were asleep, except the Tree Frog, and he scrambled out of the way as soon as he saw them coming, because he thought they might want a late supper.

"This isn't any fun!" said the brother. "Let's go to the forest."

They went to the forest, and saw the Bats flitting in and out among the trees, and the Bats flew close to the Cranes and scared them. The Great Horned Owl stood on a branch near them, and stared at them with his big round eyes, and said, "Who? Who? Waugh-ho-oo!" Then the brother and sister stood closer together and answered, "If you please, sir, we are the Crane children."

But the Great Horned Owl kept on staring at them and saying "Who? Who? Waugh-ho-oo!" until they were sure he was deaf, and answered louder and louder still.

The Screech Owls came also, and looked at them, and bent their bodies over as if they were laughing, and nodded their heads, and shook themselves. Then the Crane children were sure that they were being made fun of, so they stalked away very stiffly, and when they were out of sight of the Owls, they flew over toward the farmhouse. They were not having any fun at all yet, and they meant to keep on trying, for what was the good of being naughty if they didn't?

They passed Horses and Cows asleep in the fields, and saw the Brown Hog lying in the pen with a great many little Brown Pigs and one White Pig sleeping beside her. Nobody was awake except Collie, the Shepherd Dog, who was sitting in the farmyard with his nose in the air, barking at the moon.

"Go away!" he said to the Crane children, who were walking around the yard. "Go away! I must bark at the moon, and I don't want anybody around." They did not start quite soon enough to please him, so he dashed at them, and ran around them and barked at them, instead of at the moon, until they were glad enough to fly straight home to the place where their father and mother were sleeping with their heads under their wings.

"Are you going to tell them?" asked the brother.

"I don't know," answered the sister. When morning came, they looked tired, and their father and mother seemed so worried about them that they told the whole story.

"We didn't care so very much about what we did," they said, "but we thought it would be fun to be naughty."

The father and mother looked at each other in a very knowing way. "A great many people think that," said the mother gently. "They are mistaken after all. It is really more fun to be good."

"Well, I wish the Gulls wouldn't scream, 'Goody-goody' at us," said the brother.

"What difference does that make?" asked his father. "Why should a Crane care what a Gull says?"

"Why, I--I don't know," stammered the brother. "I guess it doesn't make any difference after all."

The next day when the Crane children were standing in the edge of the pond, a pair of young Gulls flew down near them and screamed out, "Goody-goody!"

Then the Crane brother and sister lifted their heads and necks and opened their long bills, and trumpeted back, "Baddy-baddy!"

"There!" they said to each other. "Now we are even."

THE OLDEST DRAGON-FLY NYMPH

When the Oldest Dragon-Fly Nymph felt that the wings under her skin were large enough, she said good-bye to her water friends, and crawled slowly up the stem of a tall cat-tail. All the other Dragon-Fly Nymphs crowded around her and wished that their wings were more nearly ready, and the larvae talked about the time when they should become Nymphs. The Oldest Nymph, the one who was going away, told them that if they would be good little larvae, and eat a great deal of plain food and take care not to break any of their legs, or to hurt either of their short, stiff little feelers, they would some day be fine great Nymphs like her. Then she crawled slowly up the cat-tail stem, and when she drew the tenth and last joint of her body out of the water, her friends turned to each other and said, "She is really gone." They felt so badly about it that they had to eat something at once to keep from crying.

The Oldest Nymph now stopped breathing water and began to breathe air. She waited to look at the pond before she went any farther. She had never seen it from above, and it looked very queer to her. It was beautiful and shining, and, because the sky above it was cloudless, the water was a most wonderful blue. There was no wind stirring, so there were no tiny waves to sparkle and send dancing bits of light here and there. It was one of the very hot and still summer days, which Dragon-Flies like best.

A sad look came into the Nymph's great eyes as she stood there. "The pond is beautiful," she said; "but when one looks at it from above, it does not seem at all homelike." She shook her three-cornered head sadly, and rubbed her eyes with her forelegs. She thought she should miss the happy times in the mud with the other children.

A Virgin Dragon-Fly lighted on the cat-tail next to hers. She knew it was a Virgin Dragon-Fly because he had black wings folded over his back, and there were shimmering green and blue lights all over his body and wings. He was very slender and smaller than she. "Good morning," said he. "Are you just up?"

"Yes," said she, looking bashfully down at her forefeet. She did not know how to behave in the air, it was so different from the water.

"Couldn't have a finer day," said he. "Very glad you've come. Excuse me. There is a friend to whom I must speak." Then he flew away with another Virgin Dragon-Fly.

"Hurry up and get your skin changed," said a voice above her, and there was a fine great fellow floating in the air over her head. "I'll tell you a secret when you do."

Dragon-Flies care a great deal for secrets, so she quickly hooked her twelve sharp claws into the cat-tail stem, and unfastened her old skin down the back, and wriggled and twisted and pulled until she had all her six legs and the upper part of her body out. This made her very tired and she had to rest for a while. The old skin would only open down for a little way by her shoulders, and it was hard to get out through such a small place. Next she folded her legs close to her body, and bent over backward, and swayed this way and that, until she had drawn her long, slender body from its outgrown covering.

[Illustration: SHE SWAYED THIS WAY AND THAT. Page 146]

She crawled away from the empty skin and looked it over. It kept the shape of her body, but she was surprised to find how fast she was growing slender. Even then, and she had been out only a short time, she was much longer and thinner than she had been, and her old skin looked much too short for her. "How styles do change," she said. "I remember how proud I was of that skin when I first got it, and now I wouldn't be seen in it."

Her beautiful gauzy wings with their dark veinings, were drying and growing in the sunshine. She was weak now, and had them folded over her back like those of the Virgin Dragon-Fly, but, as soon as she felt rested and strong, she meant to spread them out flat.

The fine Big Dragon-Fly lighted beside her. "How are your wings?" said he.

"Almost dry," she answered joyfully, and she quivered them a little to show him how handsome they were.

"Well," said he. "I'll tell you the secret now, and of course you will never speak of it. I saw you talking with a Virgin Dragon-Fly. He may be all right, but he isn't really in our set, you know, and you'd better not have anything to do with him."

"Thank you," she said. "I won't." She thought it very kind in him to tell her.

He soon flew away, and, as she took her first flight into the air, a second Big Dragon-Fly overtook her. "I'll tell you a secret," said he, "if you will never tell."

"I won't," said she.

"I saw you talking to a Virgin Dragon-Fly a while ago. You may have noticed that he folded his wings over his back. The Big Dragon-Flies never do this, and you must never be seen with yours so."

"Thank you," she said. "I won't. But when they were drying I had to hold them in that way."

"Of course," said he. "We all do things then that we wouldn't afterward."

Before long she began egg-laying, flying low enough to touch her body to the water now and then and drop a single egg. This egg always sank at once to the bottom, and she took no more care of it.

A third Big Dragon-Fly came up to her. "I want to tell you something," he said. "Put your head close to mine."

She put her head close to his, and he whispered, "I saw you flying with my cousin a few minutes ago. I dislike to say it, but he is not a good friend for you. Whatever you do, don't go with him again. Go with me."

"Thank you," said she, yet she began to wonder what was the matter. She saw that just as soon as she visited with anybody, somebody else told her that she must not do so again. Down in the pond they had all been friends. She wondered if it could not be so in the air. She rubbed her head with her right foreleg, and frowned as much as she could. You know she couldn't frown very much, because her eyes were so large and close together that there was only a small frowning-place left.

She turned her head to see if any one else was coming to tell her a secret. Her neck was very, very slender and did not show much, because the back side of her head was hollow and fitted over her shoulders. No other Dragon-Fly was near. Instead, she saw a Swallow swooping down on her. She sprang lightly into the air and the Swallow chased her. When he had his beak open to catch her as he flew, she would go backward or sidewise without turning around. This happened many times, and it was well for her that it was so, for the Swallow was very hungry, and if he had caught her--well, she certainly would never have told any of the secrets she knew.

The Swallow quite lost his patience and flew away grumbling. "I won't waste any more time," he said, "on trying to catch somebody who can fly backward without turning around. Ridiculous way to fly!"

The Dragon-Fly thought it an exceedingly good way, however, and was even more proud of her wings than she had been. "Legs are all very well," she said to herself, "as far as they go, and one's feet would be of very little use without them; but I like wings better. Now that I think of it," she added, "I haven't walked a step since I began to fly. I understand better the old saying,

'Make your wings save your legs.' They certainly are very good things to stand on when one doesn't care to fly."

Night came, and she was glad to sleep on the under side of a broad leaf of pickerel-weed. She awakened feeling stupid and lazy. She could not think what was the matter, until she heard her friends talking about the weather. Then she knew that Dragon-Flies are certain to feel so on dark and wet days. "I don't see what difference that should make," she said. "I'm not afraid of rain. I've always been careless about getting my feet wet and it never hurt me any."

"Ugh!" said one of her friends. "You've never been wet in spots, or hit on one wing by a great rain-drop that has fallen clear down from a cloud. I had a rain-drop hit my second right knee once, and it has hurt me ever since. I have only five good knees left, and I have to be very careful about lighting on slippery leaves."

It was very dull. Nobody seemed to care about anybody or anything. The fine Big Dragon-Flies, who had been so polite to her the day before, hardly said "Good morning" to her now. When she asked them questions, they would say nothing but "Yes" or "No" or "I don't know," and one of them yawned in her face. "Oh dear!" she said. "How I wish myself back in the pond where the rain couldn't wet me. I'd like to see my old friends and some of the dear little larvae. I wish more of the Nymphs would come up."

She looked all around for them, and as she did so she saw the shining back-shell of the Snapping Turtle, showing above the shallow water. "I believe I'll call on him," she said. "He may tell me something about my old friends, and anyway it will cheer me up." She lighted very carefully on the middle of his back-shell and found it very comfortable. "Good morning," said she. "Have you--"

"No," snapped he. "I haven't, and I don't mean to!"

"Dear me," said she. "That is too bad."

"I don't see why," said he. "Is there any particular reason why I should?"

"I thought you might have just happened to," said she, "and I should like to know how they are."

"What are you talking about?" snapped he.

"I was going to ask if you had seen the Dragon-Fly children lately," she said. And as she spoke she made sure that she could not slip. She felt perfectly safe where she was, because she knew that, no matter how cross he might be, he could not reach above the edges of his back-shell.

"Well, why didn't you say so in the first place," he snapped, "instead of sitting there and talking nonsense! They are all right. A lot of the Nymphs are going into the air to-day!" Now that he had said a few ugly things, he began to feel better natured. "You've changed a good deal since the last time I saw you."

"When was that?" asked she.

"It was one day when I came remarkably near sitting down on a lot of you Dragon-Fly children," he chuckled. "You were a homely young Nymph then, and you stuck out your lower lip at me."

"Oh!" said she. "Then you did see us?"

"Of course I did," answered he. "Haven't I eyes? I'd have sat down on you, too, if I hadn't wanted to see you scramble away. The larvae always are full of mischief, but then they are young. You Nymphs were old enough to know better."

"I suppose we were," she said. "I didn't think you saw us. Why didn't you tell us?"

"Oh," said the Snapping Turtle, "I thought I'd have a secret. If I can't keep a secret for myself, I know that nobody can keep it for me. Secrets can swim faster than any fish in the pond if you once let them get away from you. I thought I'd better not tell. I might want to sit on you some other time, you know."

"You'll never have the chance," said she, with a twinkle in her big eyes. "It is my turn to sit on you." And after that they were very good friends--as long as she sat on the middle of his shell.

THE EELS' MOVING-NIGHT

The Eels were as different from the Clams as people well could be. It was not alone that they looked unlike, but that they had such different ways of enjoying life. The Clams were chubby people, each comfortably settled in his own shell, which he could open or shut as he chose. They never wanted to live anywhere else, or to get beyond the edges of their own pearl-lined shells.

The Eels were long, slender, and slippery people, looking even more like snakes than they did like fishes. They were always careful to tell new acquaintances, though, that they were not even related to the snakes. "To be sure," they would say, "we do not wear our fins like most fishes, but that is only a matter of taste after all. We should find them dreadfully in the way if we did." And that was just like the Eels--they were always so ready to explain everything to their friends.

They were great talkers. They would talk about themselves, and their friends, and the friends of their friends, and the pond, and the weather, and the state of the mud, and what everything was like yesterday, and what it would be likely to be like to-morrow, and did you really think so, and why? The Water-Adder used to say that they were the easiest people in the pond to visit with, for all one had to do was to keep still and look very much interested. Perhaps that may have been why the Clams and they were such good friends.

The Clams, you know, were a quiet family. Unless a Clam was very, very much excited, he never said more than "Yes," "No," or "Indeed?" They were excellent listeners and some of the most popular people in the pond. Those who were in trouble told the Clams, and they would say, "Indeed," or "Ah," in such a nice way that their visitor was sure to leave feeling better. Others who wanted advice would go to them, and talk over their plans and tell them what they wanted to do, and the Clams would say, "Yes," and then the visitors would go away quite decided, and say, "We really didn't know what to do until we spoke to the Clams about it, but they agree with us perfectly." The Clams were also excellent people to keep secrets, and as the Eels were forever telling secrets, that was all very well.

Mother Eel was fussy. She even said so herself. And if a thing bothered her, she would talk and talk and talk until even her own children were tired of hearing about it. Now she was worrying over the pond water.

"I do not think it nearly so clean as it was last year," she said, "and the mud is getting positively dirty. Our family are very particular about that, and I think we may have to move. I do dread the moving, though. It is so much work with a family the size of mine, and Mr. Eel is no help at all with the children."

She was talking with Mother Mud Turtle when she said this, and the little Eels were wriggling all around her as she spoke. Then they began teasing her to go, until she told them to swim away at once and play with the young Minnows. "I'm afraid I shall have to go," said she, "if only on account of the children. I want them to see something of the world. It is so dull in this pond. Were you ever out of it?" she asked, turning suddenly to Mrs. Mud Turtle.

"Oh, yes," answered she. "I go quite often, and one of my sons took a very long trip to the meadow. He went with some boys. It was most exciting."

[Illustration: SHE WAS TALKING WITH MOTHER MUD TURTLE. Page 160]

"Is that the one with the--peculiar back-shell?" asked Mother Eel.

"Yes," replied Mother Mud Turtle sweetly. "He is very modest and does not care to talk about it much, but I am really quite pleased. Some people travel and show no sign of it afterward. One would never know that they had left home (Mother Eel wondered if she meant her), but with him it is different. He shows marks of having been in the great world outside."

Mother Eel wriggled a little uneasily. "I think I must tell you after all," she said. "I have really made up my mind to go. Mr. Eel thinks it foolish, and would rather stay here, but I am positive that we can find a better place, and we must consider the children. He thinks he cares as much for them as I do, yet he would be willing to have them stay here forever. He was hatched here, and thinks the pond perfect. We get to talking about it sometimes, and I say to him, 'Mr. Eel, where would those children be now if it were not for me?'"

"And what does he say then?" asked the Mud Turtle Mother.

"Nothing," answered Mother Eel, with a smart little wriggle. "There is nothing for him to say. Yes, we shall certainly move. I am only waiting for the right kind of night. It must not be too light, or the land people would see us; not too dark, or we could not see them. And then the grass must be dewy. It would never do for us to get dry, you know, or we should all be sick. But please don't speak of this, dear Mrs. Turtle. I would rather leave quietly when the time comes."

So the Mud Turtle Mother remembered that it was a secret, and told nobody except the Mud Turtle Father, and he did not speak of it to anybody but the Snapping Turtle.

"Did you say that it was a secret?" asked the Snapping Turtle.

"Yes," said the Mud Turtle Father, "It is a great secret."

"Humph!" said the Snapping Turtle. "Then why did you tell me?"

That same day when the Stickleback Father came to look for nineteen or twenty of his children who were missing, Mother Eel told him about her plans. "I thought you would be interested in hearing of it," she said, "but I shall not mention it to anybody else."

"You may be sure I shall not speak of it," said he. And probably he would not have told a person, if it had not been that he forgot and talked of it with the Snails. He also forgot to say that it was a secret, and so they spoke freely of it to the Crayfishes and the Caddis Worms.

The Caddis Worms were playing with the Tadpoles soon after this, and one of them whispered to a Tadpole right before the others, although he knew perfectly well that it was rude for him to do so. "Now, don't you ever tell," said he aloud.

"Uh-uh!" answered the Tadpole, and everybody knew that he meant "No," even if they hadn't seen him wave his hindlegs sidewise. Of course, not having the right kind of neck for it, he couldn't shake his head.

Then the other Tadpoles and Caddis Worms wanted to tell secrets, and they kept whispering to each other and saying out loud, "Now don't you ever tell." When a Caddis Worm told a Tadpole anything, he said, "The Eels are going to move away." And when a Tadpole told a secret to a Caddis Worm, he just moved his lips and said, "Siss-el, siss-el, siss-el-siss. I'm only making believe, you know." But he was sure to add out loud, "Now don't you tell." And the Caddis Worm would answer, "Uh-uh!"

The Eel Mother also spoke to the Biggest Frog, asking him to watch the grass for her and tell her when it was dewy enough for moving. He was afraid he might forget it, and so told his sister and asked her to help him remember. And she was afraid that she might forget, so she spoke to her friend, the Green Brown Frog, about it. The Yellow Brown Frog afterward said that he heard it from her.

One night it was neither too dark nor too light, and the dew lay heavy on the grass. Then Mother Eel said to her children, "Now stop your wriggling and listen to me, every one of you! We shall move because the mud here is so dirty. You are going out into the great world, and I want you to remember everything you feel and see. You may never have another chance."

The little Eels were so excited that they couldn't keep still, and she had to wait for them to stop wriggling. When they were quiet, she went on. "All the Eels are going--your uncles and aunts and cousins--and you children must keep with the older ones. Be careful where you wriggle to, and don't get on anybody else's tail."

She led the way out of the water and wriggled gracefully up the bank, although it was quite steep at that place. "I came this way," she said, "because I felt more as though this was the way to come." She closed her mouth very firmly as she spoke. Mr. Eel had thought another way better. They had to pass through crowds of pond people to reach the shore, for everybody had kept awake and was watching. The older ones cried out, "Good-bye; we shall miss you," and waved their fins or their legs, or their tails, whichever seemed the handiest. The younger ones teased the little Eels and tried to hold them back, and told them they'd miss lots of fun, and that they guessed they'd wish themselves back in the pond again. When they got onto the shore, the Frogs and the Mud Turtles were there, and it was a long time before they could get started on their journey. One of the little Eels was missing, and his mother had to go back for him. She found that a mischievous young Stickleback had him by the tail.

When at last they were all together on the bank, the Eel Father said to his wife, "Are you sure that the Cranes and Fish Hawks don't know about our moving? Because if they did--"

"I know," she said. "It would be dreadful if they found out; and we have been so late in getting started. We shall have to stop at the very first water we find now, whether we like it or not." She lay still and thought. "I have a feeling," said she, "that we should go this way." So that way they went, dragging their yellow bellies over the ground as carefully as they could, their dark green backs with their long fringes of back fins hardly showing in the grass. It was a good thing that their skin was so fat and thick, for sometimes they had to cross rough places that scraped it dreadfully and even rumpled the tiny scales that were in it, while their long fringes of belly fins became worn and almost ragged. "If your scales were on the outside," said their father, "like those of other fishes, you wouldn't have many left."

Mother Eel was very tired and did not say much. Her friends began to fear that she was ill. At last she spoke, "I do not see," she said, "how people found out that we were to move."

"You didn't tell anybody?" said Mr. Eel.

"No indeed!" said she; and she really believed it. That was because she had talked so much that she couldn't remember what she did say. It is always so with those that talk too much.

THE CRAYFISH MOTHER

Three Stickleback Mothers and several Clams were visiting under the lily-pads in the early morning. Mother Eel was also there. "Yes," she said "I am glad to come back and be among my old friends, and the children are happier here. As I often tell Mr. Eel, there is no place like one's home. We had a hard journey, but I do not mind that. We are rested now, and travel does teach people so much. I should think you would get dreadfully tired of being in the water all the time. I want my children to see the world. Now they know grass, and trees, and air, and dry ground. There are not many children of their age who know more than they. We stayed in a brook the one day we were gone, so they have felt running water too. It was clean--I will say that for it--but it was no place for Eels, and so we came back."

There is no telling how long she would have kept on talking if she had not been called away. As soon as she left, the Sticklebacks began to talk about her.

"So she thinks we must be tired of staying in the water all the time," said one. "It doesn't tire me nearly so much as it would to go dragging myself over the country, wearing out my fins on the ground."

"Indeed?" said a Clam, to whom she turned as she spoke.

"Well, I'll tell you what I think," said another Stickleback Mother. "I think that if she didn't care so much for travel herself, she would not be dragging her family around to learn grass and trees. Some night they will be learning Owls or men, and that will be the end of them!"

"I do not believe in it at all," said the first speaker. "I certainly would not want my sons to learn these things, for they must grow up to be good nest-builders and baby-tenders. I have told their fathers particularly to bring them up to be careful housekeepers. With my daughters, it is different."

For a long time nobody spoke; then a Clam said, "What a difference there is in mothers!" It quite startled the Sticklebacks to hear a Clam say so much. It showed how interested he was, and well he might be. The Clam who brings up children has to do it alone, and be both father and mother to them, and of course that is hard work. It is hard, too, because when a little Clam is naughty, his parent can never say that he takes his naughtiness from any one else.

"And there is a difference in fathers too," exclaimed one fine-looking Stickleback Mother. "I say that a father's place is by the nest, and that if he does his work there well, he will not have much time to want to travel, or to loaf around by the shore." The Clams looked at each other and said nothing. Some people thought that the Stickleback Mothers were lazy.

Just then a Crayfish Mother came swimming slowly along, stopping often to rest. Her legs were almost useless, there were so many little Crayfishes clinging to them.

"Now look at her," said one Stickleback. "Just look at her. She laid her eggs at the beginning of last winter and fastened them to her legs. Said she was so afraid something would happen if she left them, and that this was a custom in her family anyway. Now they have hatched, and her children hang on to her in the same way."

The Crayfish Mother stopped with a sigh. "Isn't it dreadfully warm?" said she.

"We haven't found it so," answered the Sticklebacks, while the Clams murmured "No."

"Let me take some of your children," said one Stickleback. "Perhaps carrying them has made you warm and tired."

The Crayfish stuck her tail-paddles into the mud, and spread her pinching-claws in front of her family. "Oh no, thank you," said she. "They won't be contented with any one but me."

"That must make it hard for you," said another Stickleback politely. She was thinking how quickly she would shake off the little Crayfishes if they were her children.

"It does," answered their mother. "It is hard, for I carried the eggs on my legs all through the cold weather and until it was very warm again; and now that they are hatched, the children hang on with their pinching-claws. Still, I can't bear to shake them off, poor little things!" She held up first one leg and then another to show off her dangling babies.

"I don't know what will happen to them when I cast my shell," said she. "I shall have to soon, for I can hardly breathe in it. My sister changed hers some time ago, and her new one is getting hard already."

"Oh, they'll be all right," said a Stickleback cheerfully. "Their fathers tell me that my children learn remarkably fast how to look out for themselves."

"But my children can't walk yet," said the Crayfish Mother, "and they don't know how to swim."

"What of that?" asked a Stickleback, who was beginning to lose her patience. "They can learn, can't they? They have eight legs apiece, haven't they, besides the ones that have pincers? Isn't that enough to begin on? And haven't they tail-paddles?"

"I suppose so," said their mother, with a sigh, "but they don't seem to want to go. I must put them to sleep now and try to get a little rest myself, for the sun is well up."

The next night she awakened and remembered what the Sticklebacks had said, so she thought she would try shaking her children off. "It is for your own good," she said, and she waved first one leg and then another. When she got four of her legs free, and stood on them to shake the other four, her children scrambled back to her and took hold again with their strong little pinching-claws. Then she gave it up. "You dear tiny things!" she said. "But I do wish you would walk instead of making me carry you."

"We don't want to!" they cried; "we don't know how."

"There, there!" said their mother. "No, to be sure you don't."

The next night, though, they had to let go, for their mother was casting her shell. When it was off she lay weak and helpless on the pond-bottom, and her children lay around her. They behaved very badly indeed. "Come here and let me catch hold of you," cried one. "I can't walk," said another, "because I don't know how."

Some of them were so cross that they just lay on their backs and kicked with all their eight feet, and screamed, "I won't try!" It was dreadful!

The Crayfish Mother was too weak to move, and when the Wise Old Crayfish came along she spoke to him. "My children will not walk," said she, "even when I tell them to." He knew that it was because when she had told them to do things before, she had not made them mind.

"I will see what I can do," said he, "but you must not say a word." He walked backward to where they were, and kept his face turned toward their mother, which was polite of him. "Do you want the Eels to find you here?" he said, in his gruffest voice. "If you don't, you'd better run."

What a scrambling there was! In one way or another, every little Crayfish scampered away. Some went forward, some went sidewise, and some went backward. Some didn't keep step with themselves very well at first, but they soon found out how. Even the crossest ones, who were lying on their backs flopped over and were off.

The Wise Old Crayfish turned to their mother. "It is no trouble to teach ten-legged children to walk," said he, "if you go at it in the right way."

The little Crayfishes soon got together again, and while they were talking, one of their many aunts came along with all her children hanging to her legs. Then the little Crayfishes who had just learned to walk, pointed their pinching-claws at their cousins, and said, "Sh-h-h! 'Fore I'd let my mother carry me! Babies!"

TWO LITTLE CRAYFISHES QUARREL

The day after the Eels left, the pond people talked of nothing else. It was not that they were so much missed, for the Eels, you know, do not swim around in the daytime. They lie quietly in the mud and sleep or talk. It is only at night that they are really lively. Still, as the Mother Mud Turtle said, "They had known that they were there, and the mud seemed empty without them."

The larger people had been sorry to have them go, and some of them felt that without the Eels awake and stirring, the pond was hardly a safe place at night.

"I think it is a good deal safer," remarked a Minnow, who usually said what she thought. "I have always believed that the Eels knew what became of some of my brothers and sisters, although, of course, I do not know."

"Why didn't you ask them?" said a Stickleback.

"Why?" replied the Minnow. "If I had gone to the Eels and asked them that, my other brothers and sisters would soon be wondering what had become of me."

"I have heard some queer things about the Eels myself," said the Stickleback, "but I have never felt much afraid of them. I suppose I am braver because I wear so many of my bones on the outside."

Just then a Wise Old Crayfish came along walking sidewise. "What do you think about the Eels?" asked the Stickleback, turning suddenly to him.

The Crayfish stuck his tail into the mud. He often did this when he was surprised. It seemed to help him think. When he had thought for a while, he waved his big pinching-claws and said, "It would be better for me not to tell what I think. I used to live near them."

This showed that the Wise Old Crayfish had been well brought up, and knew he should not say unpleasant things about people if he could help it. When there was need of it, he could tell unpleasant truths, and indeed that very evening he did say what he thought of the Eels. That was when he was teaching some young Crayfishes, his pupils. Their mother had brought up a large family, and was not strong. She had just cast the shell which she had worn for a year, and now she was weak and helpless until the new one should harden on her. "It is such a bother," she said, "to keep changing one's shell in this way, but it is a comfort to think that the new one will last a year when I do get it."

While their mother was so weak, the Wise Old Crayfish amused the children, and taught them things which all Crayfishes should know. Every evening they gathered around him, some of them swimming to him, some walking forward, some sidewise, and some backward. It made no difference to them which way they came. They were restless pupils, and their teacher could not keep them from looking behind them. Each one had so many eyes that he could look at the teacher with a few, and at the other little Crayfishes with a few more, and still have a good many eyes left with which to watch the Tadpoles. These eyes were arranged in two big bunches, and, unless you looked very closely, you might think that they had only two eyes apiece. They had good ears, and there were also fine smelling-bristles growing from their heads. The Wise Old Crayfish sometimes said that each of his pupils should sit in a circle of six teachers, so that he might be taught on all sides at once.

"That is the way in which children should learn," he said, "all around at once. But I do the best I can, and I at least teach one side of each."

This evening the Wise Old Crayfish was very sleepy. There had been so much talking and excitement during the day that he had not slept so much as usual; and now, when he should have been wide awake, he felt exceedingly dull and stupid. When he tried to walk, his eight legs stumbled over each other, and the weak way in which he waved his pinching-claw legs showed how tired he was.

After he had told his pupils the best way to hold their food with their pinching-claws, and had explained to them how it was chewed by the teeth in their stomachs, one mischievous little fellow called out, "I want to know about the Eels. My mother would never let me go near them, and now they've moved away, and I won't ever see them, and I think it's just horrid."

"Eels, my children," said their teacher, "are long, slender, sharp-nosed, slippery people, with a fringe of fins along their backs, and another fringe along their bellies. They breathe through very small gill-openings in the backs of their heads. They have large mouths, and teeth in their mouths, and they are always sticking out their lower jaws."

"And how do--" began the Biggest Little Crayfish.

"Ask me that to-morrow," said their teacher, stretching his eight walking legs and his two pinching-claw legs and his tail paddles, "but remember this one thing:--if you ever see an Eel, get out of his way. Don't stop to look at him."

"We won't," said one little Crayfish, who thought it smart to be saucy. "We'll look to stop at him." All of which meant nothing at all and was only said to annoy his teacher.

They scrambled away over the pond-bottom, upsetting Snails, jiggling the young Clams, and racing with each other where the bottom was smooth. "Beat you running backward!" cried the Saucy Crayfish to the Biggest Little Crayfish, and they scampered along backward in the moonlit water. There was an old log on the bottom of the pond, and they sat on that to rest. The Biggest Little Crayfish had beaten. "I would like to see an Eel," said he.

"I'd like to see them running on the land," said the saucy one.

"Pooh!" said the biggest one. "That's all you know! They don't run on land."

"Well, I guess they do," replied the saucy one. "I know as much about it as you do!"

"Eels swim. They don't run," said the biggest one. "Guess I know!"

"Well, they don't swim in air," said the saucy one. "That's the stuff that lies on top of the water and the ground, and people can't swim in it. So there!"

"Well, I've seen the Wild Ducks swim in it! They swim with their legs in the water, and with their wings in the air," said the biggest one.

"I don't believe it," said the saucy one. "Anyhow, Eels run on land."

"Eels swim on land," said the biggest one.

"Eels run!"

"Eels swim!"

"Run!"

"Swim!"

Then the two little Crayfishes, who had been talking louder and louder and becoming more and more angry, glared at each other, and jerked their feelers, and waved their pinching-claws in a very, very ugly way.

They did not notice a great green and yellow person swimming gently toward them, and they did not know that the Eels had come back to live in the old pond again. Mother Eel opened her big mouth very wide. "On land," she said decidedly, as she swallowed the Biggest Little Crayfish, "Eels wriggle." Then she swallowed the Saucy Crayfish.

"There!" said she. "I've stopped that dreadful quarrel." And she looked around with a satisfied smile.

THE LUCKY MINK

During the warm weather, the Minks did not come often to the pond. Then they had to stay nearer home and care for their babies. In the winter, when food was not so plentiful and their youngest children were old enough to come with them, they visited there every day. It was not far from their home.

The Minks lived by a waterfall in the river, and had burrows in the banks, where the young Minks stayed until they were large enough to go out into the world. Then the fathers and mothers were very busy, for in each home there were four or five or six children, hungry and restless, and needing to be taught many things.

They were related to the Weasels who lived up by the farmyard, and had the same slender and elegant bodies and short legs as they. Like the Weasels, they sometimes climbed trees, but that was not often. They did most of their hunting in the river, swimming with their bodies almost all under water, and diving and turning and twisting gracefully and quickly. When they hunted on land, they could tell by smelling just which way to go for their food.

The Minks were a very dark brown, and scattered through their close, soft fur were long, shining hairs of an even darker shade, which made their coats very beautiful indeed. The fur was darker on their backs than on the under part of their bodies, and their tapering, bushy tails were almost black. Their under jaws were white, and they were very proud of them. Perhaps it was because they had so little white fur that they thought so much of it. You know that is often the way--we think most of those things which are scarce or hard to get.

There was one old Mink by the river who had a white tip on his tail, and that is something which many people have never seen. It is even more uncommon than for Minks to have white upper lips, and that happens only once in a great while. This Mink was a bachelor, and nobody knew why. Some people said it was because he was waiting to find a wife with a white tip on her tail, yet that could not have been, for he was too wise to wait for something which might never happen. However it was he lived alone, and fished and hunted just for himself. He could dive more quickly, stay under water longer, and hunt by scent better than any other Mink round there. His fur was sleeker and more shining than that of his friends, and it is no wonder that the sisters of his friends thought that he ought to marry.

When the Minks visited together, somebody was sure to speak of the Bachelor's luck. They said that, whatever he did, he was always lucky. "It is all because of a white tip on his tail," they said. "That makes him lucky."

The young Minks heard their fathers and mothers talking, and wished that they had been born with white tips on their tails so that they could be lucky too. Once the Bachelor heard them wishing this, and he smiled and showed his beautiful teeth, and told them that it was not the tip of his tail but his whole body that made him lucky. He did not smile to show his teeth, because he was not at all vain. He just smiled and showed his teeth.

[Illustration: USED TO FOLLOW HIM AROUND. Page 191]

There was a family of young Minks who lived at the foot of the waterfall, where the water splashed and dashed in the way they liked best. There were four brothers and two sisters in this family, and the brothers were bigger than the sisters (as Mink Brothers always are), although they were all the same age. One was very much larger than any of the rest, and so they called him Big Brother. He thought there was never such a fine Mink as the Bachelor, and he used to follow him around, and look at the tip on his tail, and wish that he was lucky like him. He wished to be just like him in every way but one; he did not want to be a bachelor.

The other young Minks laughed at Big Brother, and asked him if he thought his tail would turn white if he followed the Bachelor long enough. Big Brother stood it very patiently for a while; then he snarled at them, and showed his teeth without smiling, and said he would fight anybody who spoke another word about it. Minks are very brave and very fierce, and never know when to stop if they have begun to fight; so, after that, nobody dared tease Big Brother by saying anything more about the Bachelor. Sometimes they did look at his tail and smile, but they never spoke, and he pretended not to know what they meant by it.

A few days after this, the Bachelor was caught in a trap--a common, clumsy, wooden trap, put together with nails and twine. It was not near the river, and none of his friends would have found him, if Big Brother had not happened along. He could hardly believe what he saw. Was it possible that a trap had dared to catch a Mink with a white-tipped tail? Then he heard the Bachelor groan, and he knew that it was so. He hurried up to where the trap was.

"Can't you get out?" said he.

"No," said the Bachelor. "I can't. The best way to get out is not to get in--and I've gotten in."

"Can't you do something with your lucky tail to make the trap open?" asked Big Brother.

"I could do something with my teeth," answered the Bachelor, "if they were only where the tip of my tail is. Why are Minks always walking into traps?" He was trying hard not to be cross, but his eyes showed how he felt, and that was very cross indeed.

Then Big Brother became much excited. "I have good teeth," said he, "Tell me what to do."

"If you will help me out," said the Bachelor, "I will give you my luck."

"And what shall I do with the tail I have?" asked the young Mink, who thought that the Bachelor was to give him his white-tipped tail.

"Never mind now," answered the Bachelor, and he told the young Mink just where to gnaw. For a long time there was no sound but that of the young Mink's teeth on the wood of the trap. The Bachelor was too brave to groan or make a fuss, when he knew there was anybody around to hear. Big Brother's mouth became very sore, and his stomach became very empty, but still he kept at work. He was afraid somebody would come for the trap and the Mink in it, before he finished.

"Now try it," said he, after he had gnawed for quite a while. The Bachelor backed out as far as he could, but his body stuck in the hole. "You are rumpling your beautiful fur," cried the young Mink.

"Never mind the fur," answered the Bachelor. "I can smooth that down afterward. You will have to gnaw a little on this side." And he raised one of his hind feet to show where he meant. It was a beautiful hindfoot, thickly padded, and with short partly webbed toes, and no hair at all growing between them. The claws were short, sharp, and curved.

Big Brother gnawed away. "Now try it," said he. The Bachelor backed carefully out through the opening and stood there, looking tired and hungry and very much rumpled.

"You are a fine young Mink," said he. "We will get something to eat, and then we will see about making you lucky."

They went to the river bank and had a good dinner. The Bachelor ate more than Big Brother, for his mouth was not sore. But Big Brother was very happy. He thought how handsome he would look with a white-tipped tail, and how, after he had that, he could surely marry whoever he wished. It was the custom among his people to want to marry the best looking and strongest. Indeed it is so among all the pond people, and that is one reason why they care so much about being good-looking. It is very hard for a young Mink to have the one he loves choose somebody else, just because the other fellow has the bushiest tail, or the longest fur, or the thickest pads on his feet.

"Now," said the Bachelor, "we will talk about luck. We will go to a place where nobody can hear what we say." They found such a place and lay down. The Bachelor rolled over three times and smoothed his fur; he was still so tired from being in the trap. Then he looked at the young Mink very sharply.

"So you want my tail?" said he.

"You said you would give me your luck," answered Big Brother, "and everybody knows that your luck is in your tail."

The Bachelor smiled. "What will you do with the tail you have?" said he.

"I don't know," answered Big Brother.

"You wouldn't want to wear two?" asked the Bachelor.

"Oh, no," answered Big Brother. "How that would look!"

"Well, how will you put my tail in place of yours?" asked the Bachelor.

"I don't know," answered the young Mink, "but you are so wise that I thought you might know some way." He began to feel discouraged, and to think that the Bachelor's offer didn't mean very much after all.

"Don't you think?" said the Bachelor slowly, "don't you think that, if you could have my luck, you could get along pretty well with your own tail?"

"Why, yes," said the young Mink, who had begun to fear he was not going to get anything. "Yes, but how could that be?"

The Bachelor smiled again. "I always tell people," said he, "that my luck is not in my tail, and they never believe it. I will tell you the secret of my luck, and you can have luck like it, if you really care enough." He looked all around to make sure that nobody was near, and he listened very carefully with the two little round ears that were almost hidden in his head-fur. Then he whispered to Big Brother, "This is the secret: always do everything a little better than anybody else can."

"Is that all?" asked the young Mink.

"That is enough," answered the Bachelor. "Keep trying and trying and trying, until you can dive deeper, stay under water longer, run faster, and smell farther than other Minks. Then you will have good luck when theirs is poor.

You will have plenty to eat when they are hungry. You can beat in every fight. You can have sleek, shining fur when theirs is dull. Luck is not a matter of white-tipped tails."

The more the young Mink thought about it, the happier he became. "I don't see that I am to have your luck after all," said he. "When I have learned to do everything in the very best way, it will be luck of my own."

"Of course," answered the Bachelor. "Then it is a kind of luck that cannot be lost. If I carried mine in the tip of my tail, somebody might bite it off and leave me unlucky."

Big Brother kept the secret, and worked until he had learned to be as lucky as the Bachelor. Then he married the person he wanted, and she was very, very handsome. It is said that one of their sons has a white-tipped tail, but that may not be so.

THE PLAYFUL MUSKRATS

One warm day in winter, when some of the pussy-willows made a mistake and began to grow because they thought spring had come, a party of Muskrats were visiting in the marsh beside the pond. All around them were their winter houses, built of mud and coarse grasses. These homes looked like heaps of dried rushes, unless one went close to them. If one did that, he could plainly see what they were; and if one happened to be a Muskrat, and could dive and go into them through their watery doorways, he would find under the queer roof of each, a warm, dry room in which to pass the cold days.

"Fine weather!" said every Muskrat to his neighbor. "Couldn't sleep all of such a day as this." They spoke in that way, you know, because they usually sleep in the daytime and are awake at night.

"We wish it would always be warm weather," said the young Muskrats. "What's the use of winter?"

"Hard to tell," answered one Muskrat, who had lived in the marsh longer than the rest. "Hard to tell: I know it always gives me a good appetite, though." Then all the Muskrats laughed. They were a jolly, good-natured company, and easy to get along with. The other pond people liked them much better than they did their neighbors, the Minks. The Wild Ducks who nested in the sedges, were quite willing that the young Muskrats should play with their children, and the Mud Hens were not afraid of them. Mud Hens cannot bear Minks. They say that when a Mud Chicken is missing from the nest, there is quite sure to be a Mink somewhere near with a full stomach and down around the corners of his mouth.

Perhaps if the Wild Ducks and the Mud Hens were raising their families in the winter time it might be different, for then the Muskrats get hungry enough to eat almost anything. In spring and summer, when they can find fresh grasses and young rushes, or a few parsnips, carrots, and turnips from the farmers' fields, other animals are quite safe. In the winter they live mostly on roots.

"Fine day!" screamed the Gulls, as they swept through the air. "Pity the Frogs don't come out to enjoy it!"

"Yes, great pity," chuckled the old Muskrat. "How glad you would be to see them!" He smiled all around his little mouth and showed his gnawing teeth. He knew that the Frogs were better off asleep in the mud at the bottom of the pond, than they would be sitting in the sunshine with a few hungry Gulls above them. The Turtles were sleeping all winter, too, in the banks of the pond. The Eels were lying at the bottom, stupid and drowsy, and somewhere the Water-Adders were hidden away, dreaming of spring. Of all the birds who lived by the water, only the Gulls were there, and they were not popular. It is true that they helped keep the pond sweet and clean, and picked up and carried away many things which made the shore untidy, still, they were rude, and talked too loudly, and wore their feathers in such a way that they looked like fine large birds, when really they were lean and skinny and small. The other pond people said that was just like them, always pretending to be more than they really were.

Fifteen young Muskrats, all brothers and sisters, and all born the summer before, started off to look at the old home where they were children together. That is to say, they were not all there at once, but there were five born early in the season; and when they were old enough to look out for themselves, five more came to live in the old nest; and when these were old enough to leave the nest, another five were born.

It doesn't mean so much to Muskrats to be brothers and sisters as it does to some people, still they remembered that they were related, and they played more with each other than with those young Muskrats who were only their cousins or friends. Their mother was very proud of them, and loved to watch them running around on their short legs, and to hear them slap their long, scaly tails on the water when they dove. They had short, downy fur, almost black on the back, soft gray underneath, and a reddish brown everywhere else. There was very little fur on their tails or on their feet, and those parts were black.

These fifteen children had been fairly well brought up, but you can see that their mother had many cares; so it is not strange if they sometimes behaved badly. In some other families, where there were only nine or ten babies all the season, they had been brought up more strictly. Like all young Muskrats, they were full of fun, and there were few pleasanter sights than to see them frolicking on a warm moonlight evening, when they looked like brown balls rolling and bounding around on the shore or plunging into the water. If they had all been exactly the same age, it would have been even pleasanter, for the oldest five would put on airs and call the others "the children"; and the next five would call the youngest five "babies"; although they were all well grown. There was no chance for the youngest five to call other Muskrats "babies," so when they were warm and well fed and good-natured they laughed and said, "Who cares?" When they were cold and hungry, they slapped their tails on the ground or on the water and said, "Don't you think you're smart!"

When they got to talking so and their mother heard it, she would say, "Now, children!" in such a way that they had to stop. Their father sometimes slapped them with his tail. Teasing is not so very bad, you know, although it is dreadfully silly, but when people begin by teasing they sometimes get to saying things in earnest--even really hateful, mean things. And that was what made the Muskrat father and mother stop it whenever they could.

Now the whole fifteen crowded around the old summer home, and some of them went in one way, and some of them went in another, for every

Muskrat's summer house has several burrows leading to it. When they reached the old nest at the end, all of them tried to get in at once, and they pushed each other around with their broad little heads, scrambled and clutched and held on with their strong little feet. Five of them said, "It's our turn first. We're the oldest." And five more said, "Well, it's our turn next anyway, 'cause we're next oldest." The others said, "You might give up to us, because we're the youngest."

They pushed and scrambled some more, and one of the youngest children said to one of the oldest, "Well, I don't care. I'm just as big as you are" (which was so). And the older one answered back, "Well, you're not so good-looking" (which was also true).

Then part of the brothers and sisters took sides with one, and part took sides with the other. What had been a lovely frolic became an unpleasant, disgraceful quarrel, and they said such things as these:

"'Fore I'd make such a fuss!"

"Who's making any more fuss than you are, I'd like to know?"

"Oh, yes. You're big enough, but you're just as homely as you can be. So there!"

"Quit poking me!"

"You slapped your tail on my back!"

"I'm going to tell on you fellows!"

"I dare you to!"

"Won't you catch it though!"

And many more things which were even worse. Think of it. Fifteen young Muskrats who really loved each other, talking like that because they couldn't decide whether the oldest or the youngest or the half-way-between brothers and sisters should go first into the old nest. And it didn't matter a bit who was oldest or who was youngest, and it never would have happened had it not been for their dreadful habit of teasing.

Just as they had become very hot and angry, they heard their mother's voice say, "Now, children!" but they were too much excited to mind, and they did not stop until their father came and slapped them with his tail. Then they kept still and listened to their mother. She told them that they should leave the place at once, and not one of them should even set foot in the old nest. "Suppose somebody had gotten hurt," she said. This made the young Muskrats look very sober, for they knew that the Muskrat who is hurt in winter never gets well.

After she had let them think about this for a while, she said, "I shall punish you all for this." Then there was no quarrel among her children to see who should have the first turn--not at all.

One young Muskrat said, "Aren't you going to let us play any more?"

"Yes," said she. "I shall let you play all the rest of the day, but I shall choose the games. The oldest five will play 'Mud Turtles in winter,' the next five will play 'Frogs in winter,' and the youngest five will play 'Snakes in winter.' The way to play these games is to lie perfectly still in some dark place and not say a word."

The young Muskrats looked at each other sorrowfully. They thought it sounded very much the same as being sent to bed for being naughty. They did not dare say anything, for they knew that, although their mother was gentle, as Muskrats are most of the time, she could be very severe. So they went away quietly to play what she had told them they must. But it was not much fun to play those games when all the others were having a fine time in the sunshine.

There were nine of the young Muskrats who did not tease any after that. Even the other six were more careful.

###

Made in the USA
Las Vegas, NV
12 November 2024